Ira M. Millstein

THE

ACTIVIST

DIRECTOR

Lessons from the Boardroom and
the Future of the Corporation

Columbia University Press
Publishers Since 1893
New York   Chichester, West Sussex
cup.columbia.edu
Copyright © 2017 Ira M. Millstein LLC.
All rights reserved

Library of Congress Cataloging-in-Publication Data
Names: Millstein, Ira M., author.
Title: The activist director : lessons from the boardroom
and the future of the corporation / Ira Millstein.
Description: New York : Columbia University Press, [2017] |
Series: Columbia Business School publishing | Includes index.
Identifiers: LCCN 2016031218 | ISBN 9780231181341
(cloth : alk. paper)
Subjects: LCSH: Boards of directors—United States. | Directors of
corporations—United States. | Corporate governance—United States. |
Corporations—Investor relations—United States.
Classification: LCC HD2745 .M527 2016 | DDC 658.4/22—dc23
LC record available at https://lccn.loc.gov/2016031218

Columbia University Press books are printed on permanent
and durable acid-free paper.
Printed in the United States of America

Cover design: Noah Arlow

CONTENTS

CONTENTS

INTRODUCTION

I was asked by a director of a client company to counsel his wife, who was a brilliant board member of a Fortune 500 corporation. Members of her board sought to replace the CEO, whom they considered incapable of doing his job. However, they did not believe they could remove him. I advised them that they not only had the authority, but also the responsibility, to oversee, and replace when necessary, management. They just needed to reject the board's traditionally passive and deferential role. They did so, marched into the CEO's office, and told him that he was fired. The CEO's response: "You can't do that." The directors, flustered, left his office and called me for advice. I counseled them to go back to the CEO's office and explain that they were empowered by law to replace him. They did so, and to their amazement, the CEO left.

Next I was asked to counsel directors of foreign corporations on improving access to global capital. I focused on the importance of directors creating a system of transparency, honesty, and integrity to encourage the flow of capital.

This included management oversight. The directors believed they were doing their jobs according to the book. I asked them to raise their hands if they thought they could fire the CEO. Not one hand went up. I told them they weren't yet adequate directors, just passive people controlled by management.

The stories I tell are not just lessons I taught directors. They were eye-opening lessons for me. Many directors still don't understand their roles and responsibilities as fiduciaries of corporations.

What makes this passive mindset so dangerous to the future of our corporations, and to us? Simply, today's corporations face global competition and require access to global capital. These are the facts of life under which corporations must operate, innovate, and grow. Yet too many directors cater to the short-term boosting of share price, and become slaves to the quarterly capitalism of earnings guidance and analyst estimates. Under pressure, they forgo innovation and growth. Some short-term thinking is needed to earn long-term gain—but not so short-term that it hobbles a company's ability to achieve the long-term. That's what's happened to the American corporation.

Many pundits told us not to worry, that in the long run the magic of our free market system would self-correct and, if we were patient, all would be well without interventions by government, pesky shareholders, or meddlesome directors. The theory didn't work. Being patient is not the answer—our current competitive positions don't improve; indeed, they continue to erode in too many areas with no concrete solutions for improvement.

We need a fundamental change in corporate leadership. Passivity must become the past. We must elect directors who will steer our corporations to be the vigorous competitors they are capable of being, able to attract long-term capital. I wrote this book to drive a stake into passivity.

Throughout this book I use the term *capital market* to encompass the zoo of pension funds, mutual funds, hedge funds, private equity, program traders, investment advisors, and the host of other financial services. Too many of them want to prosper quickly, failing to focus on your long-term security.

The key to breaking this unvirtuous circle is, I believe, how the corporation is governed. The story I will tell is based on my own experience over fifty years practicing law—advising corporations on governance matters, prodding and urging directors to take action, and working behind the scenes (and sometimes on stage and in court). This included counseling, among others, General Motors, American Express, Westinghouse, Macy's, Drexel Burnham Lambert, Mayor Abraham Beame and New York City during the fiscal crisis, Con Edison, Planned Parenthood, the Organization for Economic Cooperation and Development, the New York State Task Force on Pension Fund Investment, and the New York State Commission on Public Authority Reform. A board of directors is at the epicenter of the affairs of the corporation and caring for its well-being, not just by law, but also as a practical matter. The board is your representative to deal with the pressures of the capital market. Board centricity is your protection.

If corporate governance worked perfectly, corporations would operate efficiently and transparently, creating value for their shareholders. This would happen within the limits set by law.

Right now it's not working very well. The list is long and well known: the Enrons and WorldComs who misled shareholders with accounting gimmicks; the banks and housing market manipulators who almost collapsed the entire financial system; manufacturers with misleading practices that cost billions in penalties and damages.

I place the problem at the foot of boards of directors who shirk their responsibility to manage the future of the corporation for your benefit.

Important, too, are the hedge funds and activist institutions that cause share movements by simply asserting the need for change. The media and the proxy advisors (who are not fully informed, because they are rarely, if ever, present in the boardroom) do the rest, then a herd of other stockholders follow, sensing an opportunity for profits through short-term price swings. These people treat shares of stock like casino chips.

Where were the corporate boards in these situations?

The solution, I believe, is not more regulation. Whatever regulations have piled up over the years are easily overcome by those who have the ingenuity. Regulation follows a crisis—it deals with what has happened. It cannot deal with what will happen.

Management and other beneficiaries will use questionable practices to apply short-term pressure to move the corporation's stock. Corporate boards must resist those who seek illusory short-term gains at the cost of the corporation's value as a whole. They must balance the need for some short-term gains with the overriding need to create long-term value for shareholders.

In this book, I will chart how we ended up where we are today, examining real-world examples from my years of legal involvement with corporate governance failures that were caused by little or no serious board-centric oversight. I will build the case for adopting a board-centric approach to corporate governance by placing more *activist directors* in the boardroom—people who will ask the tough questions, challenge management practices, and resist those who put their own agendas ahead of those of the corporation and investors like you. Choosing directors will require new diligence and care.

Some will call this pie-in-the-sky idealism. I prefer to call it pragmatic optimism. There is no easy fix that will correct these flaws, but this book outlines the steps to bridging the short and long terms.

EARLY YEARS

"The scientist discovers that which exists. An engineer creates that which never was."
—Theodore von Kármán, founder of Aerojet
and Jet Propulsion Laboratory

My fascination with how corporations worked began after I accidentally flooded the basement of the Columbia University engineering school in 1944.

I was measuring the torque of a one-horsepower engine with big flywheels that had to be kept cool with water to avoid overheating. If you turned it off in a hurry, the flywheel would stop and the water would come pouring out. There was a protocol for slowing it down and gradually withdrawing the water, but I ignored it. Suddenly water was cascading all over the floor and it took me, a janitor, and several mops to clean up the mess. That's when I switched to industrial engineering from electrical engineering. I eventually gave up that major because I didn't understand electricity.

I grew up in New York in the 1930s. Both sets of Polish-German grandparents had emigrated to the United States in the late 1800s. My paternal grandfather was a cabinetmaker who spoke mostly Yiddish. He wore spats. It was rumored that he was a womanizer, and he spent a short time in debtor's prison. My mother's father Americanized, and even became an alderman—a Republican, no less. He ran a cigar store in the Bronx, which I visited on the weekends, marveling at the wealthy people who arrived to pick up boxes of cigars that had been hand-rolled in the back room. My mother's brother ran away from home and became a Texas Ranger because he couldn't stand my grandmother.

The Depression haunted us. My father, at one point a successful furniture salesman, lost his showroom in Manhattan and spent the rest of his professional life on the road, selling bedroom sets and living room furniture to stores in little towns throughout the Northeast. He was an outstanding salesman, and I know I learned "how" by watching him. This was an especially tough job during the war, when lumber was badly needed for military construction.

We lost our house in New Rochelle to the banks, and adjusted to apartment living in Manhattan. Gone were some of the friends, clothes, and trips for the family. When the first apartment on West 85th became too expensive, we moved again to a cheaper apartment farther uptown on West 99th Street.

Both were perfectly adequate places to live, and we never stood in a breadline. But it was upsetting to be uprooted twice within a relatively short time, which, in the life of a young person, embeds itself deep in the memory. I have been concerned about money ever since, hence my natural instinct to fear potential financial disasters and to seek stability. I had only two real jobs after law school—at the Department of Justice and at Weil, Gotshal & Manges (65 years and counting).

My childhood home was dysfunctional because of the Depression and the war. One of my brothers-in-law died in an Air Force raid in the Far East, the other served years overseas in the field artillery.

I tried to be the mediator of the family—my parents and two older sisters, Lucille and Marcia. I thought I saw all sides. I also tried to mediate the street fights that happened all too frequently. Tough Irish kids from Amsterdam Avenue sometimes invaded our largely Jewish neighborhood, particularly around Easter, and attacked with silk stockings filled with sand and pebbles, shouting anti-Semitic slurs. When reasoning failed, we fought back; however, it was nothing more than typical street scuffles—no knives or guns involved. We were all chastised when the police intervened and called our mothers. That did it, and peace reigned—until the next time.

Though my efforts proved futile at home and in my neighborhood, the discipline of negotiating compromise has remained. I try to see all sides of a problem and find solutions. I wasn't very successful as a kid, but the process of trying stuck with me.

To distance myself, I focused on school, and, as was not unusual in those days, I leapfrogged grades so that I was ready for high school at thirteen years old.

I entered The Bronx High School of Science as a freshman in 1940. Bronx Science was founded only a year earlier as a "selective" New York City public school, with outstanding teachers and a challenging array of seminars rather than traditional classes. The school gave me both a physical and mental escape into a world of intellectual stimulation that didn't exist in my home. We studied not just science and math (up to advanced calculus), but French, civics, history, and typing. In class we discussed politics, current events, history, and philosophy—our debates were lively, even intense, and I gained the confidence to argue compellingly about what I believed, and to beware of ideology.

I was accepted to Columbia in 1943, in part because I was on the swimming team at Bronx Science, even though my team lost most of our meets. I think being Jewish helped me get admitted. It was common practice at the time at all the Ivy League schools to limit the number of Jewish students to 10 percent of the class. I made the cut when I promised the director of admissions I'd try out for the swim team. I apparently helped fill the Jewish quota by being otherwise useful.

At just sixteen, I entered Columbia. World War II demanded fresh troops, so the student body was shifting every day. I started out in the college's well-known liberal arts program that focused on the classics, history, and art, but after a year I switched to engineering to take advantage of my experience at Bronx Science. And I thought that if I were called up to serve in World War II, an engineering degree would help me on the road to becoming an officer. The war years deprived me of a real college experience—wallowing in philosophy, great books, and just thinking. I've tried to catch up ever since. Outside of class, I ran the food concession at the Baker Field football stadium with my friend Bill Canahan. On a particularly hot day we filled empty coffee urns with water, sugar, and a little lemon juice—then Bill turned off the stadium drinking fountains. Our lemonade sold very well. They didn't let students run the concession after that. I learned that not all entrepreneurship was socially acceptable.

Not wanting to be left out of World War II, I left Columbia during my second year to enlist in the Army. I was seventeen. Later I was honorably discharged after a bad asthma attack, which likely saved my life by putting me back on campus to finish up engineering school. But to my dismay, I missed combat.

Banned from the engineering labs for destroying equipment and failing to understand thermodynamics, I found a welcome niche in industrial engineering, which I did understand. My new major introduced me to Professor Walter Rautenstrauch, whose 1943 book *Principles of Modern Industrial Organization* I read again and again. The book explained the engineer's view of the organization of the modern corporation. It was a machine with moving parts:

directors, managers, employees, suppliers, production lines, and so on. Its fuel was capital, supplied by the shareholders and banks. Fascinated by that simplicity, I thought the financial sector was secondary to the work of the world, if I thought about it at all.

I did well in Law for Engineers, a course taught by Assistant Dean James Gifford from Columbia Law School. He took a liking to me and would soon play an important role in securing my place at the law school, but not before I tried unsuccessfully to be an industrial engineer. The war was ending, and companies like General Electric, where I wanted to work, were laying off rather than hiring. So I went to work in a furniture factory in Rahway, New Jersey, that made some of the furniture my father sold on the road. I was miserable. My job was to design a conveyor belt system that would speed up the painting process of cabinets, which was then done by a group of men standing around spraying them. I had absolutely no interest in time-clocking what these people were doing, or in figuring out how to do it better. It didn't seem human. So I quit after three months, returned to Morningside Heights, and looked for Dean Gifford.

I didn't think I had the grades at engineering school (mostly Cs) that would warrant admission to a law school such as Columbia's, but after taking an aptitude test and getting a lot of help from Dean Gifford, I was admitted to Columbia Law School. Because of my interest in the workings of corporations, he urged me to take a job as assistant to Professor Milton Handler, the legendary antitrust expert who advised FDR and co-drafted landmark statutes such as the National Labor Relations Act.

Professor Handler was a tough taskmaster. I did everything—buying his cigarettes, getting coffee and sandwiches, anything he wanted. My legal work, helping him with his casebook "Trade Regulation," was to read England's case law up to about the 1400s to trace the beginnings of trade restraints. I came away with a deep understanding that open competition in markets was a must from the very beginning of a society. Many would try anything to avoid competition, by fixing prices with competitors or forestalling their entry to the market. These unsophisticated restraints became more sophisticated as economies matured, but the object was still the same: eliminate competition wherever possible.

Working with Professor Handler was torturous, but I learned. In helping him brief cases more recent than 1400, and some current ones, he would make me analyze over and over until he was satisfied. "That isn't what I asked you for," he would say. "I want to know why you are reading this case and what I asked you to look for." I rewrote one memo a dozen times. What he was looking for was the definition of the market that a steelmaker was part of. When I described it too simply, he'd say, "No, no, no. What were they doing? What was their business? Who were the competitors? You didn't read the case!"

Professor Handler was teaching me an art: how to extract the nugget from a pile of slurry—and then attack it. He taught me how to write lean and not wander. This skill would serve me going forward, especially in partner meetings planning strategies for monster cases at Weil, Gotshal & Manges. I'd say, "How are we going to prepare for this? What do we really want to do? We're not just taking deposition or discovery. What is it we're looking for? Why are we doing this? Do we have to do it? Are there other things we ought to be doing? Before we go too far, we've got to find out what the core of our strategy is and why we are doing this."

Professor Handler backed me for a job in the Antitrust Division of the Department of Justice when I graduated in 1949. Those two years in Washington remain a highlight of my career. I felt proud walking across the mall, entering the Department of Justice building, and going to work in the library. Docents conducting tours would say, "Those are Justice Department lawyers working on important cases."

One case I worked on charged Timken Roller Bearing Co. with conspiring with a British and a French firm to allocate trade territories among themselves, fix prices on antifriction bearings, and protect each other's markets from outside competition. The case went up to the U.S. Supreme Court, who sided with the original charges: Timken had violated the Sherman Antitrust Act.

Another case was American Can, charged with tying the sale of cans to the leasing of can-closing machines at little or no cost. The leasing scheme eliminated competitors trying to sell cans. The case ended in a dramatic result, forbidding tie-ins between the selling of cans and can-closing machinery, and created a more competitive market.

When the division head left to start his own firm and invited me to join him, I thought of leaving Washington altogether. I went to see John Lord O'Brian, a partner at Covington & Burling, a firm with great legal force in Washington. O'Brian asked me, "Are you afraid of government?"

I said I wasn't. Then it was time to go, he told me: I had learned what I needed to know about the government.

I started my search in New York, ready to get my hands dirty in actual practice with clients and courts. Standing behind the Justice Department banner in courtrooms seemed to me an unfair test of litigation skill. I was still too young to be chosen by law firms for major antitrust cases or, for that matter, any antitrust cases. Those were the provinces of the white-shoe Wall Street firms that too often did not welcome Jews. I had learned that on graduation from law school.

But this time, with the Justice Department pedigree, interviewing was easier. Rosenman & Colin offered me a job, but when the hiring partner told me I'd be in the library for some years before I saw a client, I declined. I chose Weil, Gotshal & Manges instead, where I was told I could immediately have more responsibility. I have been with Weil for over sixty years, and it was at Weil that I counseled the mayor of New York City during the fiscal crisis, investigated Con Edison after the blackout, advised the boards of General Motors, Planned Parenthood, and Drexel, drafted fiduciary duty concepts into law, and experienced all the other stories in this book.

THE ACTIVIST DIRECTOR

1

A MESS THAT CAN'T BE FIXED?

What is this mess we find ourselves in? When did it begin, and how did it get worse? How complicated is it? The essentially free financial market invents and improvises equity and debt instruments. These instruments may positively raise capital but at the same time hurt growth and innovation. Can we strike a balance?

This chapter surveys the panorama of our changing capital market. In brief terms it will explain how the market became so complex, its changing fads, arcane deals and practices, and financial instruments. It may sound confusing, because it is.

The current mess had no single tipping point. There was no conspiratorial meeting at some remote Adirondack camp where investment bank and hedge fund managers declared once and for all that individual shareholders were henceforth irrelevant. No one decided that our simple model of capital-raising was outmoded or that corporate directors must now redirect their attention from managing the corporation to playing defense. No one considered, "How much money should be diverted in the coming quarter from R&D

spending into dividends or stock buybacks to satisfy institutional pressure for stock price gains, board seats, the CEO's head, or the breakup of the company? After all, we did miss earnings guidance by two cents a share last quarter."

There were also no detailed plans to derail the long-term interests of shareholders—those who provided the fuel of capital to begin with—who hoped their investments would be used to grow not only the corporation, but also their own financial futures.

Yet here we are. But how did we arrive?

It was a cavalcade of questionable decisions: a concentration of power in intermediaries like major banking institutions, pension funds, and "wolf packs" of activist hedge funds who acquire shares under the radar; the advent of high-frequency trading; and the emergence of "dark pools," private stock markets run inside financial firms that pit the holdings of ordinary shareholders against high-frequency traders. Then there's the mindset of mutual funds and pension funds that tend to measure themselves by their peer groups and thus focus on the short term so they don't fall behind in attracting capital; the timid and entrenched boards that are captive, at one time or another, to management or proxy advisors or both; and the unintended consequences of regulators who fix the system, only to find that their solutions have opened new avenues to exploit shares.

All of this creates a major challenge for corporate boards to recruit the best possible directors—men and women of good character and exceptional experience and competence, who are willing to devote time to define the company's vision (what the company wants to be) and mission (how to get there), who are willing to question management closely, and who are strong enough to fend off those who seek "change" for their own benefit. I will discuss this further in the last chapter.

For now, multiply this set of challenges by five thousand—the number of companies listed on public exchanges in the United States—and it's not hard to see why the so-called economic recovery is fragile. How did the capital markets structure go from something relatively simple to something extraordinarily complex? If even the experts find it difficult to understand what's really going on, how can the individual investor?

The twenty-four-hour media coverage doesn't help—its megaphone amplifies the tiniest divergence from "guidance" in an earnings report. It's a storyline reinforced by senatorial voices of authority, even though these pundits have little, if any, inside knowledge of the company. Rarely, if ever, are they in the boardroom to report that what seems like a misstep is part of a sound long-term strategy. But the markets react accordingly. The relentless flow of data and news bewilders rather than clarifies. In the words of former British Prime Minister James Callaghan, "A lie can make its way around the world before the truth has the chance to put its boots on."

No wonder shareholders are uneasy about the capital markets and their investments. And, by the way, *who are* the shareholders of corporate America these days?

Individual shareholders have often been left behind, misled, or "herded" to their detriment. The problem has been with us from the start. Charles Mackay in *Extraordinary Popular Delusions*, first published in 1841, described the

Mississippi Scheme, the South Sea Bubble, and Tulipomania, all examples of misled investors. Change the dates and the names, and you have a template for Enron, WorldCom, and the 2008 bust.

The South Sea Company was founded around 1711 as a joint-stock company with a monopoly granted over British trade in South America. But when the Treaty of Utrecht ended the War of Spanish Succession and acknowledged Spain's claim to South America, the South Sea Company was left without trading prospects. In January 1720 the company was stagnating. To inflate the price of the stock, the directors of the South Sea Company published rumors that the company was successfully trading in the endless bounty of South America. By June the share price had increased tenfold. But investors had no idea that very few ships had set sail. The whole enterprise was a fraud. Investors, who couldn't be fed on rumors forever, started selling shares in July. In August the stock collapsed back to its January rate, devastating the English markets. Prosecutions of major company and government officials followed. The downside of public ownership of the corporation was becoming clear. If you ask individual shareholders today, my guess is they won't think things are much better—they perceive a lack of transparency and accountability to shareholders.

The New World imported the British concept of the corporation, but it evolved differently here. In America the corporation could behave as an individual person, entering into binding commercial contracts while shielding the people who formed it from most personal liability. The limited liability of the shareholder was a critical hook to fundraising, but at the same time, it motivated excessive risk-taking. From the beginning, the states handled corporate law, since it was in their interests to advance liberal provisions that would bring in capital and promote economic growth. They competed for the business of incorporation.

The New York Stock Exchange was formed by a group of bankers in downtown Manhattan in 1792. At the beginning, independent share ownership was fairly dispersed and insignificant in early capital creation, with the later exception of railroad, steel, auto, and oil companies that created monopolies and lush rewards for Leland Stanford, John D. Rockefeller, and Henry Ford.

After fits and starts, the number of share owners gradually increased in the 1920s. They took a nervous pause during the Depression, came crawling back afterward, and their numbers exploded after World War II when the veterans returned, eager for their piece of the American Dream. The economy was strong, corporate profits were rising, there was virtually no inflation, and bond yields were low. Equities were a sound investment. Investing seemed to be the right thing to do.

But a major survey commissioned in 1956 by the New York Stock Exchange found that only a little over 4 percent of the population owned common stocks. The Big Board thought that percentage was far too low. Brokers weren't making sufficient commissions, since "turnover"—the rate at which shares changed hands—was feeble during the fifties, not even close to what we see today. Something had to be done, and NYSE President G. Keith Funston thought he had just the answer: broaden the market to attract people who had never before owned stocks.

So began a vigorous fourteen-year campaign called "Own Your Share of American Business." It mobilized a massive public relations and advertising effort that used every marketing tool available: the slogan was used in millions of newspaper and magazine advertisements, and it was posted on company bulletin boards and supermarket checkout counters. It was even displayed prominently in department store windows. The Big Board, working with advertising agencies and marketing consultants, created marketing programs like "Invest in America" weeks to garner attention.

The NYSE pushed the Federal Reserve to relax margin requirements to stimulate individual share ownership. According to the Business History Conference, the Own Your Share program "was designed to disassociate equity investing from its negative gambling connotation and instead inflate it to a patriotic act that blended citizens' self-interest with the national interest."

It worked. By 1965, ownership percentage had more than tripled to 15 percent of people owning shares. Today, Gallup estimates that 55 percent of "retail" (individual) shareholders invest in the stock market, down from the peak of 65 percent just before the 2008 meltdown, but holding relatively steady ever since.

To the extent that shareholders in the early years of this buying spree were "activists," such efforts were mostly confined to individual shareholders who owned one hundred or fewer shares. Some individual shareholders owned just a few shares so they could attend annual meetings. One well-known shareholder who garnered a lot of attention, Evelyn Y. Davis, particularly enjoyed needling the International

Telephone & Telegraph Corporation's CEO, Harold Geneen, loudly asking at annual meetings how executive compensation was determined and who counted the shareholder votes. Sometimes her microphone would fail for "unexplained technical reasons."

Imperial CEOs hoped these people would just go away, but they didn't. Not knowing how to deal with vocal shareholders, companies turned to outside public relations firms or proxy solicitors to handle annual reports and orchestrate "feel good" annual meetings that offered food and open bars. But these third parties weren't always familiar with the inner workings of corporations, so some of the public relations efforts included overtly promotional material, which came perilously close to stock touting. Lawyers were getting nervous.

Companies wanted more control. In 1953 General Electric took the lead in a new field by establishing an investor relations department with its own executives. This department eventually expanded to deal with security analysts as well. Other companies followed suit, and the American Management Association launched a series of conferences to promote the field. There was now a mechanism in place to deal with both individual shareholders and a growing number of intermediaries—like mutual funds and pensions—in which individuals were investing. These institutions were dominating American share ownership.

By 1950, twenty-two states had adopted the Prudent Man Rule, which allowed fiduciary institutions like pension funds to invest substantial assets in common and preferred stocks. Pension funds grew rapidly, increasing in value from $11 billion to almost $40 billion between 1950 and 1957.

Today, pension funds control more than $20 trillion in assets worldwide, and mutual fund holdings are over $16 trillion.

Institutions like these own at least 60 percent of the largest one thousand U.S. corporations. Ownership of substantial interests in the vast majority of U.S. corporations is concentrated in fewer than a dozen intermediaries—firms like BlackRock, State Street, Fidelity, and Vanguard.

That's a sobering thought. It suggests a concentration of asset ownership that looks and feels a lot like what the American founders hoped to avoid. The dispute between Alexander Hamilton and Thomas Jefferson was fundamentally about concentrated financial power, with England at the core. Jefferson was concerned about the growing power of the early corporations, in which he saw the potential for the creation of a new American feudalism. Discussing the fall of the British aristocracy in an 1816 letter, Jefferson wrote, "I hope we shall take warning from the example and crush in its birth the aristocracy of our monied corporations which dare already to challenge our government to a trial of strength and bid defiance to the laws of our country."

But the trend continued. For instance, starting in the 1970s brokerage firms encouraged clients to keep their stock in "street name," the name of the brokerage firm in which stock is held on behalf of a purchaser.

Some found the idea of "street name" shareholding unsettling. But they could point to no specific reason for their concerns, and soon gave in to the convenience of selling shares with a phone call instead of a trip to the bank vault. Of course the brokers liked it. It was a more efficient system that could generate more trades and heftier commissions.

Today, some (including gold advocate James Sinclair) warn that the small investor who goes along with the street-name option imperils his holdings by allowing the broker to lend shares to a short seller or borrow money against them to speculate in the derivatives market. Sinclair, warning of the 2011 collapse of commodity futures broker MF Global, said, "These hidden risks are the seeds of tomorrow's ultimate collapse of broker dealers which could dissipate the assets of customer accounts." MF Global allegedly improperly transferred almost $900 million of customer funds to cover trading losses and liquidity shortfalls at subsidiary units.

The power of concentrated stock ownership reached a peak in the "Greed is Good" 1980s, with its takeovers, insider trading, and the 23 percent drop of the Dow in October 1987.

There was enough ownership in fewer hands for "shareholders" to rock the corporate board and even take over a corporation. It was no longer necessary to reach out to thousands of individual shareholders. Controlling shareholders saw takeovers as a cure for corporate underperformance and passive boards. These takeovers seemed like a good idea to many at the time. It woke up boards who were possible takeover targets. But the takeovers didn't work. Too often they were merely expensive and disruptive ways to bring in a new CEO, with no assurance that he or she wouldn't break up the company.

The acquired company often struggled under the enormous debt that had largely funded the takeover. Boards of potential targets started playing defense, adopting poison pills or creating large conglomerates with no strategic logic, to gain some degree of protection. These were not long-term strategies for the welfare of the corporation. These board-adopted defenses did, however, support the idea of boards being empowered to do what they deemed to be in the best interests of the corporation. Beginning in the 1980s, and continuing today, courts have upheld poison pills as a valid response to hostile takeover bids if the board shows it was acting against a threat to the corporation and its actions were reasonable in relation to the threat posed.

The borrowed money used to purchase a company in a leveraged buyout (LBO) is often paid back through reducing workforce or selling off pieces of the company. These LBOs became particularly fashionable during the 1980s. The time was ripe for it: target valuations were relatively low, leverage was available, and there was an inventory of companies to be picked off the shelves.

LBO volume in the 1980s totaled $285 billion, including the $3.1 billion KKR takeover of RJR Nabisco, which inspired the book and movie *Barbarians at the Gate*. Other noteworthy buyouts included Carl Icahn's hostile takeover of TWA, Canadian real estate developer Robert Campeau's purchase of Federated Department Stores, and the LBO of Thatcher Glass, financed in part by over $100 million in bank loans at an interest rate of 22.5 percent. All of these companies, unable to handle the staggering debt payments, ended in bankruptcy. LBOs, resulting in concentrated ownership in the hands of a few shareholders, became the means to advance risky ventures.

Shareholders turned to growing intermediaries for capital to fund their activism.

My involvement with shareholder activists and concentrated ownership began shortly after General Motors bought Electronic Data Systems (EDS) in 1984. EDS was the big data processing company owned by the feisty Ross Perot, who joined the GM board as part of the deal. Perot clashed with CEO Roger Smith and other directors, who were offended by Perot's habit of complaining to the press about the board. Perot would often drop by my office and complain about how little the board did. But directors reported that *he* did nothing in the boardroom to raise or resolve the issues that concerned him.

GM wound up buying out Perot's GM stock at a more than 80 percent premium and he left the board. But Perot didn't stop complaining about GM, telling *Fortune* in 1988 that the General Motors system was like

> a blanket of fog that keeps these people from doing what they know needs to be done. I come from an environment where, if you see a snake, you kill it. At GM, if you see a snake, the first thing you do is go hire a consultant on snakes. Then you get a committee on snakes, and then you discuss it for a couple of years. The most likely course of action is— nothing. You figure, the snake hasn't bitten anybody yet, so you just let him crawl around on the factory floor. We need to build an environment where the first guy who sees the snake kills it.

Perot was not like the activist of today. But he was a concentrated owner who attracted attention.

Many institutional investors were sympathetic to Perot's complaints about the shortcomings of GM management. When Perot's shares were bought back and he was removed from the board, big investors sold off GM stock—enough to cause a 10 percent drop in value in a matter of days.

When the Council of Institutional Investors invited Perot and Smith to present their sides of the dispute to members, Perot showed up but Smith did not. The State of Wisconsin Investment Board proposed a shareholder resolution to be voted on at the GM annual meeting. The resolution protested the Perot buyout and sought to amend the company's bylaws to prohibit such transactions. That attracted Roger Smith's attention. He finally met with some of the big public pension funds. The Wisconsin group withdrew its support of the resolution, but the flap was an important moment: it showed the potential proxy power of big investors.

Investors concerned with the inequities of the market had their fears realized on October 19, 1987. The markets dropped a stomach-wrenching 23 percent on a day that would be later branded Black Monday, echoing the first day of the 1929 crash. The Dow collapsed 508 points.

Continuing a decline that began the prior week, the high volume of sell orders overwhelmed the systems at the opening bell Monday morning, and floor specialists couldn't open for an hour. Confusion and panic spread through cash and futures markets. Wells Fargo reportedly sold thirteen installments of just under $100 million each, $1.1 billion in one day.

This, the biggest percentage drop in stock market history—equivalent to 3,600 points today—prompted a rare two-column headline on the front page of *The Wall Street*

Journal the next day: "The Crash of '87: Stocks Plunge 508 Amid Panicky Selling." (The only other time the paper altered its sober six-column front-page format was to report the start of the war on Japan after Pearl Harbor. The *Journal* reported the first day of the October 1929 crash with the understated one-column headline, "Market Orderly in Record Drop.")

While some worried that the 1987 crash could plunge the country into recession, economists generally dismissed this notion—and luckily they were right. Stocks rebounded the next day, posting a record gain of 102.27 points on the Dow. Another rally followed on Wednesday, signaling the beginning of a bull market that would last another decade.

Even though that Tuesday ended on an up note, it was "the most dangerous day we had in fifty years," said Lazard Frères & Co. general partner Felix Rohatyn. "I think we came within an hour [of a disintegration of the stock market]," he told the *Journal*. "The fact we didn't have a meltdown doesn't mean we didn't have a breakdown. Chernobyl didn't end the world, but it sure made a terrible mess."

That day, securities firms and floor specialists found that the banks they normally depended on for loans were cutting back badly needed credit. Many stocks—like IBM, Merck, and DuPont—couldn't open or else closed quickly. Specialists didn't have any buy orders. The Chicago Board Options Exchange closed because so many options weren't trading. The New York Stock Exchange itself seriously considered closing, a step that would have sent a profoundly troubling signal to the world's markets.

In the end, only a flood of liquidity from the Federal Reserve and a concerted effort by big companies to buy back their stock (prompted by frantic calls from their investment banks), and an odd but fortuitous spike in futures on the Major Market Index (traded on the Chicago Board of Trade) brought the markets back from the brink.

Though they did not cause the crash, two relatively new elements of market structure contributed to the volatility: program trading and portfolio insurance. Program trades are large-volume transactions that are typically executed automatically when index prices rise or fall to predetermined levels. Portfolio insurance is a hedging technique used by institutional investors to mitigate market risk by short-selling stock index futures. Both are unpredictable and trigger volatility.

The 1987 panic roused investors' worst fears and sent a sobering message to the directors of the corporations whose combined market valuations shed a stunning $500 billion that day. The complexities of a vastly changed capital markets environment were at work. This environment relied not on thoughtful assessments of the soundness of corporate fundamentals, but rather on automated trading algorithms and an unsettling concentration of ownership by intermediaries, whose own priorities often clashed with those of primary investors who seek long-term capital appreciation. The unsuspecting public was left behind.

Disruptive advances in technology were yet to come. Today, high-frequency traders with algorithms and fiber optic speed enable intermediaries to serve their own interests rather than the investors and corporations the market is meant to serve. Michael Lewis's *Flash Boys*, which unsurprisingly notes that the market is rigged, describes in detail how these traders gain timing edges measured in milliseconds, an advantage that leaves the small investor hopelessly behind.

Lewis gives prominence to the work of Eric Hunsader, whose firm Nanex takes price streams from U.S. exchanges and distributes the data through software so they can use it to write their own trading programs. Hunsader has concluded that high-frequency traders (HFTs) were the primary culprits behind the scary May 2010 "flash crash," when the industrial average fell almost 1,000 points in minutes. Hunsader says HFT firms are exploiting market rules to earn outsized profits in what he calls a "lawless environment." "Did you ever see *Lord of the Flies*?" he asked a Bloomberg reporter. "When you don't have a parent around, things fall apart."

Then, of course, came 2008. The well-known and much debated causes were the U.S. housing bubble, an explosion of mortgage-backed securities (MBSs), and collateralized debt obligations (CDOs). Millions of first-time homebuyers were lured into the market by subprime mortgages, which offered 8 percent interest for the first two years, then jumped to 15 percent for the remaining twenty-eight years. Banks approved loans for people who clearly could never pay them off. For a while, it was like printing money—making an easy spread by borrowing short-term in the money markets while buying triple-A-rated, long-term mortgage-backed securities.

Insurers played a role too, issuing "credit default swaps," insurance-like policies that underwrote losses caused by mortgage defaults. Big financial institutions bought and sold the default swaps on assets they didn't own. By 2008, the amount of credit insured by these derivatives had grown to

$62 trillion from $900 billion in 2001. Warren Buffett called the swaps "financial weapons of mass destruction."

In 2007 and 2008, as defaults began to rise, banks that had heavily invested in subprime assets—particularly the lower, more risky tranches of MBSs and CDOs—began to chalk up big losses. From there it snowballed. Bear Stearns ran out of money and was bought out by J.P. Morgan. The initial deal was $2 a share. Tense negotiations upped it to $10, valuing the company at less than the market price of the Bear's Manhattan flagship office.

Lehman, with its client base evaporating, its stock plummeting, and its credit ranking tanking, frantically approached Morgan Stanley, Bank of America, and Barclays to cut a deal. But no one would bite, and the Treasury Department failed to rescue Lehman, citing "moral hazard." So Lehman, once the fourth-largest investment bank in the United States, declared bankruptcy and sold its parts around the world at fire-sale prices. Merrill, another bank with heavy exposure to MBSs, sold itself to Bank of America. The latest boom and bust bubble burst, exacerbated by a new and complex capital market, left an unsuspecting public victimized.

Washington reacted by creating the Troubled Asset Relief Program (TARP), which bought not only assets but equity stakes in the banks, a temporary "nationalization" that unsettled just about everyone on Wall Street. Could it happen again? Of course.

Where was the oversight? Debt ran rampant. The entire financial market created debt to enable investment in the most risky adventures. Where were the boards of those granting or creating debt? Why weren't directors asking tough questions about risky underwriting practices and overextension into shaky assets? The answer was the usual one: as long as we're making money, don't ask too many questions.

One would think we learned a lesson about unrestrained debt creation, especially debt based on a risky asset like speculative real estate. We couldn't count on shareholders to see a bubble inside a complex capital market, but how about the more knowledgeable boards of those creating the risks? Weren't boards on notice about their responsibilities to the entire corporate community?

Apparently not yet.

Activist funds, particularly hedge funds—opaque, privately organized investment pools not subject to the same disclosure requirements as public corporations—have dramatically upped the pressure on corporate executives and boards. There were more than eight thousand hedge funds managing a cumulative $2.8 trillion at the end of 2014, a threefold increase in assets over a decade, according to HFR, the research outfit that tracks the industry's trend. Activist funds manage about $200 billion in assets—a mere fraction of the stock market value of American corporations. But activist leverage (debt) and influence far exceed the dollars invested when they demand board seats, CEO replacements, or strategy shifts.

The concentration of wealth in intermediaries is the fuel for activists. Without the fuel, they could not be active. So they are active.

In the first nine months of 2015, eighty-two shareholder proposals to implement proxy access—a mechanism allowing shareholders to nominate directors in the company's proxy statement—were submitted and voted upon at annual shareholder meetings. Forty-eight of these shareholder proposals, submitted by shareholders who held at least 3 percent of the voting power of the company's securities, garnered enough shareholder votes to pass. This compares with only five passed in all of 2014.

But there's no guarantee that an activist investor will suddenly transform an underperforming company into a successful one. Of particular concern these days is the hedge fund wolf pack: several funds acting not as a group but in parallel to buy up shares in a target, using the securities law to their advantage by exploiting the ten-day window between the time the "lead wolf" starts buying shares and when he is required to disclose ownership in a 13D filing with the SEC.

According to financial data company FactSet, 405 campaigns between 2001 and 2014 involved multiple parties, 220 of which included a dissident group seeking board seats. And 107 of those won at least a single board seat.

Consider the case of Darden Restaurants. In 2014 its *entire board* was replaced through the efforts of activist hedge fund Starboard Value LP, which worked alongside Barington Capital Group. During the company's annual shareholder meeting, Darden's shareholders elected all twelve of Starboard's director nominees. Darden had sold its Red Lobster chain without a shareholder vote, which a majority of shareholders had requested. Starboard argued that Darden's management had shown "contempt for shareholder interest."

And Sotheby's, the oldest company on the New York Stock Exchange, recently emerged from a bruising fight with Daniel Loeb's Third Point and other hedge funds, which forced out longtime CEO William Ruprecht. Loeb, whom Ruprecht called "scum" in an email made public at trial, secured three board seats through the confrontation. He also got Tad Smith, a new CEO thought to have a no-nonsense approach.

Besides the wolf packs, two of the most powerful U.S. institutions are flexing, publicly stating their intended future activism in governance. Vanguard, with $3 trillion in assets under management, is the largest mutual fund in the U.S. and a major shareholder in some of the biggest corporations. In a 2015 letter to several hundred public companies, CEO William McNabb wrote, "In the past, some have mistakenly assumed that our predominantly passive management style suggests a passive attitude with respect to corporate governance. Nothing could be further from the truth." In an interview with *The Wall Street Journal*, McNabb noted, "We are 5 percent of most major companies. We should be doing this. We felt like we should take it to another level."

McNabb's letter urged boards to appoint an independent chairperson, rather than a member of management, and to increase interaction with shareholders, possibly through a shareholder liaison committee. "It's more about the behavior than the framework," he told the *Journal*. "We're indifferent as to how a board chooses to engage. What's important is that it engages."

Along the same lines, BlackRock—the world's largest asset manager with $4.65 trillion in assets under management—has issued newly revised voting guidelines, signaling that it may now oppose U.S. directors' reelection over things like lengthy tenures, a year's worth of poor board attendance, lack of diversity, and inadequate board succession planning. BlackRock says it opposed 7 percent of directors last year.

Only time will tell whether these institutions will take a more active role in governance.

The perception that the table is always tilted in the house's favor in a complex capital market, in disregard of the unsuspecting public, has been reinforced over the past thirty years by rounds of insider trading crimes. Many of these were prosecuted by two high-profile U.S. attorneys for the Southern District of New York—Rudolph Giuliani in the 1980s and now Preet Bharara.

Giuliani's well-publicized targets included Ivan Boesky, Michael Milken, Marty Siegel, and Dennis Levine. In *Den of Thieves*, James B. Stewart wrote that the scope of the crimes dwarfs "any comparable financial crime, from the Great Train Robbery to the stock manipulation schemes that gave rise to the nation's securities laws in the first place. The magnitude of the illegal gains was so large as to be incomprehensive to most laymen."

Bharara prosecuted Sri Lankan hedge fund manager Raj Rajaratnam, who fielded a group of sources who fed him inside information, upon which his Galleon Funds racked up Bernie Madoff–sized returns. One of Rajaratnam's sources was Rajat Gupta, the esteemed former managing director of McKinsey & Co. and a director of Goldman Sachs, who phoned Rajaratnam minutes after learning in a Goldman board meeting that Warren Buffett was going to make a major investment in the investment bank. With the exchange closing only minutes away, Rajaratnam immediately ordered his firm to buy up Goldman shares, which rose substantially the next day.

Today activist shareholders push boards to divert funds from R&D into dividends or stock buybacks. According to a *Financial Times* analysis, the portion of cash flow allocated to repurchase for S&P 500 companies has risen to 30 percent, nearly twice what it was in 2002, while the portion allocated to capital expenditures is down to 40 percent from more than 50 percent in the early 2000s. The *Financial Times* began its story with an anecdote about a Carl Icahn letter to Apple's Tim Cook, asking him to approach his board about using more of Apple's $133 billion in cash to buy back more of its shares. Polite? Yes. Vaguely threatening? Could be perceived that way.

Larry Fink, the head of BlackRock, believes we've created a gambling culture in which we tune out everything except the most immediate outcomes. He argues that failing to invest in new capacity or new technology robs the future of "big, long-term bets that create jobs and keep an economy on top of the innovation curve." The starving of corporate investment stifles growth and amplifies inequality.

Marty Lipton, fellow lawyer and friend with whom I've sometimes sparred, has made it a personal crusade to protect corporations from activist campaigns launched in the name of shareholders. I don't always agree with Marty, but I applaud his efforts to curb short-termism in the boardroom. He stunned the investment community when he called for less emphasis on quarterly earnings guidance, an obsessive hedge fund focus where a penny's difference in reported results can trigger the sale or purchase of millions of shares. *American Lawyer* quoted an anecdote from one of Lipton's colleagues at Wachtell, Lipton, Rosen & Katz. The colleague said that over the course of three months, three separate activists threatened to "destroy" three Wachtell clients if they didn't do so-and-so. Another Wachtell lawyer said activists are "flat-out uncivil, rude, loud, and obnoxious. They are totally unpleasant and total bullies."

Can shareholders—even when they're activists—sort through the "mess" of the new capital market, and ensure the future of the corporation? Lucian Bebchuk at Harvard Law School lobbied for mandatory compensation disclosure like CEO-to-median-employee pay ratio disclosures, so shareholders can rein in extravagant CEO compensation. In fact, Bebchuk stirred up the business community with his paper, "The Long-term Effects of Hedge Fund Activists." Citing performance figures of every activist-targeted company over five years, Bebchuk claims that activists have a favorable effect on long-term performance. I don't think you can prove things simply by relying on numbers. It is important to look around and see what is actually happening in the world. We cannot place "mathematical elegance over reality," to quote Lord Adair Turner, former chair of the UK Financial Services Authority.

That, then, is a very brief and, I hope, useful sketch of the mess we are in. Despite this, we need to foster growth and innovation within our existing capital market.

How can corporate governance contribute?

We need to renew a commitment to *responsible* boards in all types of organizations, where directors are activists in the best sense of the word. In the boards I've counseled over the last half century—even those of the biggest and most prestigious companies—too often only three or four directors knew the business, were fully engaged, and did the jobs they should have been doing. We need many more of them.

2

THE BOARD-CENTRIC IMPERATIVE

B oard centricity—the central role of the board in the affairs of the corporation—keeps the corporation on its competitive toes and capable of attracting operating capital. Under the board-centric model, as required by Delaware law, boards of directors are positioned at the epicenter of all corporate affairs, entrusted as the corporation's ultimate authority. But whether or not corporations understand this seems to wax and wane. Far too often, boards have been passive, failing to question management until something goes wrong. This chapter will hop-skip through fifty years of history and explain why, as a practical, let alone legal matter, the board is central, and why the corporate community seems to take the board's role seriously only when directors are complacent. The corporate community then looks around for support. That support, we will see, has unintended consequences.

My hope is that if the public, the policy makers, and the academy get the point, the pressure will be on the corporations to recognize board centricity. Corporations can't learn through spasmodic attacks, they must ingest centricity once and for all—and, more important, seriously implement it—especially now that corporations, and their directors, are under increasing pressure from the diverse zoo of shareholders and their competing demands in an existing capital market "mess."

A corporation needs a steady hand at the helm, with commitment and courage, to keep it on course to build value. This is far preferable to more regulation or succumbing to self-seeking motivations.

As always, we start with the law. A corporation is not a human being with morals and motivations. It is a creature of the statutes that created and circumscribed it.

But why should anyone beside lawyers and academics care about board centricity? If you're a shareholder, chances are your money is not always being put to the best use. This is not because directors are incompetent or crooked. Rather, most are simply not doing their jobs properly. A director of a company in which you hold shares is your agent—as required by the statutes. The board is charged with the duty of managing the business and affairs of the corporation.

The board is there to ensure that your money is not inappropriately lining the pockets of managers or wasted on foolish ventures. Rather, it must be used to create value for the ultimate beneficiary—you.

If you help fuel a corporation's growth by buying its shares or debt directly—or more likely, through an intermediary like a brokerage firm, mutual fund, or pension fund—you expect that money to be stewarded to create long-term value.

But who really looks after your interests? Do you have any practical control of how the corporation uses your money?

As a day-to-day matter, the answer seems to be no. But through proper corporate governance, credibly and transparently practiced, the answer is a definitive yes.

Corporate governance is the system each board creates and employs to select, monitor, and compensate its managers, and to relate what it learns to shareholders.

The system varies as the board adapts statutes, judge-made law, customs, and best practices. It encompasses the relationship of directors and managers to one another, and their responsibilities to shareholders and those who depend on the corporation.

The board is the fulcrum of U.S. corporate governance between shareholders and the public on one side and managers on the other side. Directors, rather than shareholders or management, are the ones directed to manage the affairs of the corporation, including implementing sound corporate governance practices. Too often directors have either forgotten or just ignored the board-centric requirement, because of inertia or external pressures or simply because they don't understand their responsibilities.

The point of this chapter is to understand how we got where we are today—what worked and what did not work.

When corporate governance changed, its evolution was rarely self-generated, but more often precipitated by a catalyst. Changes don't come when things are good and going well. Corporations were doing well and the economy was growing during my early years of practice beginning in the 1950s and continuing for the next decade. The antitrust laws worked to keep corporations competitive, and competition weeded out the failures. Boards weren't overly active and didn't have to devise new models of governance to survive. Public management removals in large corporations were rare, if any. In my early years of practice, I can't recall a public removal of a CEO. More often it was done, if at all, beneath the radar disguised as a resignation. The closest it came was when Sewell Avery, chairman of Montgomery Ward & Company, in a labor dispute with President Franklin D. Roosevelt, was physically and visibly removed by soldiers from his office.

Antitrust regulation began with a simple market concept: there ought to be competition to provide consumers with choices in price, quality, or service. This is the core of antitrust law, ensuring competition in markets to provide consumer welfare. Beginning in 1890, the Sherman Antitrust Act and subsequent antitrust statutes were enacted as business arrangements became more and more complex. Courts quickly involved themselves in determining what behavior was "anticompetitive." Starting in the 1930s, structuralism took hold as the governing ideology. Proponents of structuralism believe that highly concentrated industries can result in collusion and discourage competition. The fewer the producers, the more incentive—and opportunity—to collude.

Structuralists endorsed laws that would remake industries if they became unduly concentrated. For example, Senator Philip Hart's 1972 "Industrial Reorganization" bill, as originally introduced, would have made it unlawful for any corporation to hold monopoly power in any line of commerce in any section of the country. The general reliance on the government went so far that special administrative agencies or courts were to be empowered to break apart an industry and rebuild it pursuant to stated legislative guidelines. Happily, that effort failed.

Americans continued to distrust power concentrated in corporations. As Supreme Court Justice William O. Douglas wrote in 1948, "Power that controls the economy . . . should be scattered into many hands so that the fortunes of the people will not be dependent on the whim or caprice, the political prejudices, the emotional stability of a few self-appointed men." The Sherman Act, he added, is "founded on a theory of hostility to the concentration in private hands of power so great that only a government of the people should have it."

Post–World War II America enjoyed a period of unbroken prosperity. The economy flourished, the stock market was rich and healthy, and there was barely any foreign competition for our domestic goods. As corporations prospered, they provided employees with unprecedented wages and consumers with an increasing array of improved products and services. Employee minimum wage rates tripled between 1938 and 1950. Major public corporations, like General Electric, General Motors, Exxon, IBM, and Sears, became household names and drove the nation's wealth.

Management was largely credited with the corporation's success. But "managerial capitalism" had unintended consequences. By the late 1970s, management largely controlled boards, whose members were now often handpicked by the managers. Boards were passive and inert, pliable rubber stamps for the decisions of imperial CEOs. Rarely did directors challenge the strategies and performance of managers. Throughout this book I will share my own experiences with counseling passive directors, including those of General Motors, Macy's, and Westinghouse. The major unintended consequence of managerial capitalism: little accountability to the owners. But public shareholders, like directors, for the most part, remained passive and uninformed.

Complacent U.S. companies were ill-equipped to face mounting foreign competition from Japan and Germany in the late 1970s through the 1980s. Boards couldn't or wouldn't respond quickly enough to change managers to remain competitive.

By the time Ronald Reagan took office in 1981, America had been through a decade of rising unemployment and inflation. There were many causes, but uncompetitive response to foreign competition was high on the list. If the American economy was to thrive again, it could not just ignore foreign competition, hoping it would go away.

This culminated in "Reaganomics," the free-market approach to economic theory and policy favored by academics like Milton Friedman of the University of Chicago and strongly embraced by Corporate America, where anti–New Deal and anti-structuralist sentiment was slowly but inexorably growing.

To promote growth, President Reagan deregulated certain key industries such as banking, cable television, long-distance phone service, and oil and gas. He believed that antitrust laws represented an unnecessary restraint. Business discretion and the market, rather than the government, should determine competition.

The Reagan era effectively embargoed the antitrust laws. They simply weren't enforced except for minor price-fixing cases for road building and so on. Gone was the restraint of enforced competition. During that time I wondered what the restraints on management might be, and I turned my attention to the boards. Were they acting as any kind of monitor on management? The answer was not really, which I found disturbing, as I was becoming less convinced that the "free market" was an effective replacement for the antitrust laws, capable of creating corporations able to compete in a now global market.

Boards were still passive. They failed to question the strategies of unchained managers who acted with abandon, growing their companies quickly and indiscriminately, making questionable deals—and ultimately floundering. Boards made no effort to understand their shareholders, particularly the growing power of the pension funds and institutional investors who were flexing their muscles and challenging management.

Recognizing the need to wake up directors and educate them on their fiduciary duties to oversee the corporation, a dedicated group of people in the 1970s and 1980s, working both independently and together, emerged to remind the corporate world of the original board-centric approach to governance.

Our objective: to ensure that boards exert some initiative to restore corporate competitiveness.

While not forming an official group, a few of us often worked together to bring about change in the boardroom. Among us were Sir Adrian Cadbury, the chocolates executive who became the change agent for governance reform in the United Kingdom; Dale Hanson, who was for many years head of the $300 billion (asset) California Public Employees' Retirement System (CalPERS), the country's largest public pension fund; and Richard Koppes, the former general counsel of CalPERS who has focused on corporate governance and shareholder value issues. I also worked with the Washington, DC–based nonprofit advocacy organization, the United Shareholders Association, founded by T. Boone Pickens in 1986 and led by Ralph Whitworth. The organization used its more than 65,000 members to sponsor proxy proposals encouraging corporations to change their governance structure.

We concluded that the traditional framework of corporate governance, based on management domination and director inertia, was ineffective. We needed a model where directors would take responsibility for what shareholders had entrusted them to do—to be central to the corporation.

One of the earliest "statement of the case" arguments for a more assertive board came in a 1934 *Harvard Law Review* article by Douglas when he was a young law professor at Yale. The future Supreme Court Justice, writing in the same year the Securities and Exchange Commission was created, described in "Directors Who Don't Direct" the "vicious practice" of a board "dominated" by managers. Such a board, he warned, is likely to "suffer from myopia and lack of perspective."

Turning this giant ship 180 degrees has been no easy feat, and I (and others) certainly don't suggest that there is not more to be done to encourage appropriate investor influence and restoration of board centricity. Yet it's worth examining those steps that have been taken to try to objectively measure the degree of their success. Of course it hasn't all been good news. For instance, the boards of Enron, Tyco, WorldCom, and, more recently, Hewlett-Packard clearly did not get our memo.

THE BUSINESS ROUNDTABLE

Interestingly, although misunderstood and sometimes maligned by those suspicious of corporate executives, the early Business Roundtable (BRT) played a major role in shaping my thinking of what must be done. In counseling the organization in the 1980s, I found some very sound thinking and imaginative plans.

Beginning in the late 1970s, as corporate economic performance was declining, shareholders started speaking up. Profits at Chrysler, for instance, were in steady decline as the company lost market share to Honda, Nissan, and Toyota. Then in 1995, Chrysler's largest shareholder, Kirk Kerkorian, launched an unwanted takeover bid to put pressure on the automaker. The effort failed, but it was a major wake-up call to the Chrysler board—and to most American CEOs.

Empowered by the free-market environment, boards embraced hostile takeovers when under pressure from shareholders to govern better. During the 1980s nearly half of all major U.S. companies received some sort of takeover offer. In 1988 alone, there were 168 hostile bids valued at $222 billion, including the bitter $30 billion battle by Kohlberg Kravis Roberts & Co. to take over Nabisco.

Any company whose numbers looked bad or whose balance sheet had flaws was a potential target. No one was safe.

But were leveraged buyouts (LBOs) and hostile takeovers the key to more effective governance? Of course not. So I worked with the BRT to reform board practices to ensure that directors were properly empowered, educated, and capable of executing strategic plans for their corporations.

I first started working with the BRT because of Reginald Jones, chairman and CEO of General Electric from 1972 to 1981. He was not only a client but also a close friend during my time counseling General Electric on such issues as the turbine generator price-fixing case. Reg was also cochairman of the BRT, and he focused their attention on the role of the board. He was one of the best CEOs and board members I have ever had the pleasure of working with. Reg long recognized the importance of the board's role at the center of corporate governance.

My partners at Weil, Gotshal & Manges and I drafted several statements on corporate governance that were published by the BRT. These statements set forth critical board responsibilities like board selection, structure and composition, management selection, and the all-important issue of succession—guidelines developed from actual experiences, not from business textbooks.

Beginning with the BRT's report in 1978, followed by other reports that used the 1978 report as their base, the BRT annunciated the guiding principles of corporate governance. (The Business Roundtable Reports include *The Role and Composition of the Board of Directors of the Large Publicly Owned Corporation* [1978], *Statement on Corporate Responsibility* [1981], *Statement of the Business Roundtable on the American Law Institute's Proposed "Principles of Corporate Governance and Structure: Restatement and Recommendations"* [1983], *Corporate Governance and American Competitiveness* [1990], and *Statement on Corporate Governance* [1997].) The report urged the business community to "reexamine intensively board operations and procedures and board composition." It addressed board composition, director independence, board committee structure, and the relationship between the CEO and chairman of the board. Specifically, adopting a board-centric approach to governance, the report stated that "the board is the ultimate corporate authority," and directors, rather than shareholders, are the ones who should manage the corporation, including determining management and board succession, considering decisions and actions that could have a major economic impact, and establishing policies and procedures to comply with the law.

The 1978 report also spelled out another important board responsibility: "the consideration of significant social impacts of corporate activities and relatedly the consideration of views of substantial groups . . . significantly affected by such activity." The report was among the first to articulate that a corporation has a responsibility not only to its shareholders, but also to society.

The 1978 report contained a key principle, one which the BRT championed well before many: *information flow.* The report claimed that it "is the board's responsibility to establish . . . systems and procedures to assure that there is a flow of information to the board sufficient to permit the effective discharge of its obligations . . . The underlying principle is that each corporate organization needs to design mechanisms to assure that the board will address and decide essential questions to assure that it has a proper basis for decision." The Roundtable Reports were not meant to offer mandatory prescriptions for directors to blindly follow. Rather, they were meant as *aspirational* guidelines. There is too much diversity in the private sector to approach corporate governance with a cookie cutter.

THE INSTITUTIONAL INVESTOR PROJECT

I hoped that the board-centric Business Roundtable Reports would encourage directors to understand and accept their responsibilities, which included recognizing shareholder needs. I hoped, too, that articles I wrote in the 1980s with the hopes of educating and vitalizing boards would wake up directors. (See e.g., Winthrop Knowlton and Ira M. Millstein, "Can the Board of Directors Help the American Corporation Earn the Immortality It Holds So Dear?" [1988]. See also Ira M. Millstein, "Institutional Activism: Why Boards of Directors Must Be Actively Involved in Corporate Pension Fund Investment Policy" [1989].) I urged directors to play a more active role in the governance of their corporations, including controlling their own meeting agendas, closely monitoring and challenging management, spending more time on their jobs and communicating effectively with shareholders.

Unfortunately, the more I counseled directors in the 1980s, the less they seemed to listen. This may have been because of director inertia, or because directors didn't understand their own responsibilities, or because of internal and external pressures, or perhaps because of a combination of all of the above. Directors had precious little contact with their shareholders. Without that, how could directors understand the concerns of the people whose investments they were entrusted to steward? It was not enough for the BRT and others to preach that "good" corporate governance practices should include open and honest dialogue between boards of directors, shareholders, and management.

If there was to be forward movement by boards, institutional shareholders had to be heard—they needed to speak up. Encouraging institutional shareholders to find their voice is what I set off to do at Columbia University.

More than eighty years ago, two Columbia Law School faculty members, Adolf A. Berle and Gardiner Means, published *The Modern Corporation and Private Property*, which characterized the separation of ownership and control that was the hallmark of the large public corporation in the United States.

But the marketplace had dramatically changed, and the Berle-Means world was no more. It was large institutional shareholders, not individuals, who owned equity.

Some wondered whether the falling performance of some iconic American corporations could be traced, even if only in part, to corporate governance, which was ill-suited to contemporary shareholder reality. These changes led many to question whether the Berle-Means–style corporation reflected the optimal corporate governance structure for all large firms.

At the heart of the changing paradigm was the "new institutional owner" of corporate America—the employee pension funds, mutual funds, insurance companies, bank trusts, brokerage firms and other similar intermediaries. They were replacing the individual as the predominant direct owner of corporate securities.

Before, a mass of individual shareholders kept their fancy-looking certificates in their safe deposit boxes, often visiting them just to hold in their hands proof that they owned part of General Motors, DuPont, or U.S. Steel.

The change in ownership was radical. Assets under management by institutional investors more than doubled in six years, from $2.1 trillion in 1981 to $4.6 trillion in 1987—and to $5.2 trillion a year later. As a group, institutional investors owned an increasingly large share of U.S. equities, holding approximately half the equity of U.S. corporations. Specifically, by 1989, institutional investors held approximately 50 percent of the equity of the top fifty corporations ranked by stock market value and 53 percent of the top hundred corporations. Interestingly, institutional investors today own in the aggregate more than 70 percent of the outstanding equity in the thousand largest U.S. corporations.

This was a watershed in corporate governance. By virtue of their concentrated economic power, institutional investors could exert more and more power over directors and managers. Gone were the days when corporations were owned by a mass of faceless shareholders. Many large institutions, while replacing individuals as the predominant owners of corporate equity, wanted to be heard by the corporations that they owned. They believed directors and management were building moats around themselves—entrenching themselves and ignoring shareholder wishes or rights.

Management, on the other hand, had for years become accustomed to making decisions without anyone second-guessing them. Many managers, espousing "managerial capitalism," believed that the only role of shareholders was to profit or to sell off their holdings when dissatisfied—what they call "taking the Wall Street Walk." Some managers even questioned whether pension fund investors were "real" stockholders, and not just politicians.

Tension mounted between institutional investors and boards of directors and corporate managers. A corporation cannot achieve long-term economic success under a crippling battle between those who manage the affairs of the corporation and those who own it. At its worst, the relationship between managers and institutional investors was hostile. At its best, it was passive, when institutions had effectively abdicated responsibility. For example, it was not uncommon to hear statements by management as made by Charles Wohlstetter, former chairman and CEO of Contel. Wohlstetter, writing about pension funds in "The Fight for Good Governance," wrote that "in sum, we have a group of people with increasing control of the Fortune '500' who have no proven skills in management, no experience at selecting directors, no believable judgment in how much should be spent for research or marketing—in fact, no experience except that which they have accumulated controlling other people's money." It had to change.

It was in the corporate community's self-interest to gain the support of long-term shareholders like the pension funds. They could be friends in warding off raiders and self-seeking short-termers, who were part of the hostile takeover, indiscriminate deal-making era.

Shareholders, boards of directors, and management should have a common goal—to position U.S. corporations to succeed in an increasingly global and competitive economy. But they didn't come together to meet this challenge. Nor could they agree upon what role institutional investors should play in this new paradigm. I knew that something had to be done to bring together institutional investors, corporate boards, and management. This required effective communication and interaction, which was almost nonexistent.

It is against this backdrop that Columbia Professor Louis Lowenstein and I established the Institutional Investor Project in 1988 at the Center for Law and Economic Studies at Columbia, in collaboration with the New York Stock Exchange and under the direction of a board of advisors composed of members of the institutional investor, business, and academic communities. They included, to name just a few, Bruce Atwater, Jonathan Charkham, Harvey Goldschmid, Jeffrey Gordon, Elmer Johnson, Reginald Jones, Richard Koppes, Philip Lochner Jr., Jay Lorsch, Carl McCall, Ned Regan, and Mark Roe.

The Institutional Investor Project broke ground in bringing together institutional investors and large corporations in a neutral forum to close the gap between investors and managers. There was substantial support, through participation in roundtables and financial contributions, from directors and management. They recognized that if they failed to build relationships with their shareholders and garner shareholder support, they were vulnerable to hostile takeovers. To me, the Institutional Investor Project was a perfect fit at Columbia, because my alma mater had been one of the leading centers for studying the corporation in the twentieth century.

The project successfully convened conferences and colloquia sessions, initiated research, and provided opportunities for dialogue between institutional investors, corporate boards, and officers. Research efforts focused on, among other things, gathering data to document the significance of institutional investors and commissioning research on institutional investor behavior, corporate responses to institutional investors, pension fund turnover and holding patterns, and the concentration of holdings and voting authority by institutional investors in U.S. corporations.

The data, periodically updated, has been heavily used by Congress, the Departments of Treasury and Labor, the Securities and Exchange Commission, and by scholars and commentators in the field. The data made it clear that directors and management could not ignore institutional investors. They were growing in size and influence at an unprecedented rate and there was no evidence of a slowdown. The result was that corporations began to, for the first time, engage with institutional investors to better understand them. Corporations were finally realizing that without effective institutional shareholder engagement, they risked increased shareholder turnover rates and hostile takeovers. My involvement with the project was and continues to be one of the most rewarding parts of my personal governance mission, providing tools for directors, management, and shareholders to better understand one another through open and honest communication.

THE NEW YORK STATE TASK FORCE ON PENSION FUND INVESTMENT

The work done at the Institutional Investor Project was certainly not limited to Columbia. The seeds we planted in thought leaders flourished in other sectors as well. In 1988 Governor Mario Cuomo set up the New York State Task Force on Pension Fund Investment, which I chaired in 1989. With "antigovernment" and "bigger is better" sentiments still running rampant, it was easier for pension funds to either support LBOs or sell their stock for a quick profit if they were unhappy with a corporation's performance. For example, by 1989, the New York State Common Retirement Fund's pension money had funded the buyout of RJR Nabisco, Duracell, Beatrice, Stop and Shop, and Safeway.

Cuomo realized that the government and the business community, including pension funds, must work together for the long-term good of corporations. Lee Smith, then the director of the task force, knew of my role as counselor to New York City during the financial crisis, and of my private practice legal representation of companies such as General Electric and General Motors. Lee also knew about my contributions to the Business Roundtable Reports. He recommended to Cuomo that I chair the task force, which was the beginning of one of many future endeavors with Cuomo.

Figure 2.1   Ira Millstein, Governor Mario Cuomo, and Daniel Walsh, President of The Business Council of New York State, during the release of *Our Money's Worth* (1989).

It was clear that pension funds were no longer passive agglomerations of assets whose investment policies had a systemic impact on our economy. The world of pension funds had become complicated, and its reach was growing. New York State's public employee pension systems alone had almost $100 billion in assets, almost one-sixth of the $658 billion total assets held by all public employee pension funds. Yet, even though pension funds were the largest single investors in our equity markets and played a key role in the allocation of capital, no one had questioned their responsibilities to the larger economy.

We could no longer accept the status quo—pension funds operating in a vacuum with the sole goal of their own returns.

Pension funds must recognize their responsibilities to promote the long-term performance of the corporations in which they invested, acting as stewards of the nation's capital. With this idea, the task force was entrusted with addressing pension funds' responsibilities. This went further than providing retirement security to its beneficiaries. It also included organizing and using capital to encourage the renewal of economic competitiveness in a global economy. More specifically, it meant that pension funds needed to play a more active role in the governance of the corporations in which they invest, including monitoring corporate performance to ensure that it is managed diligently, voting responsibly during the proxy process, and building healthy relationships with boards. The task force was the first of its kind to study the role of pension funds in the economy and in the governance of American corporations. This was no easy job. Pension funds, corporations, and the government all had a different idea of their role. The task force was a collaborative effort that spanned almost a year and consisted of representatives of public corporations and labor and public and pension funds. The task force also sponsored two days of public hearings on March 3 and March 8, 1989. Representatives of pension funds, the New York State government, financial institutions, and academics all testified.

After months of intense collaborative efforts to harmonize everyone's idea of what a pension fund should do, the task force issued its report, titled *Our Money's Worth*. The report recognized that the "extraordinary accumulation of capital by the nation's pension funds has vested in them significant ownership responsibilities with respect to America's large corporations. . . . But despite this transformation, our policies and our thinking have not significantly changed."

The report was a first-of-its-kind blueprint. The task force recognized "that pension fund trustees, as controllers of a large proportion of our available 'patient capital,' have responsibilities broader than the traditional understanding of their legal duties may indicate." Pension fund trustees had to move beyond maximizing immediate returns in every transaction, and focus on investment conduct that created stronger and more competitive corporations (and the economy) in the long term.

The task force urged pension funds that wielded such power in our equity markets to consider the full effect of their actions when formulating and implementing their investment and ownership policies. We made several specific recommendations and outlined the importance of fund trustees (on behalf of pension fund beneficiaries) voting for the board of directors in the corporations in which they invest. We believed that fund trustees could back directors who would best protect the interests of their pension fund beneficiaries. The report leveraged my previous efforts at urging the Council of Institutional Investors, to whom I spoke with on several occasions, to move away from focusing on their option to sell their investments, taking the "Wall Street Walk." Instead, they ought to exercise their rights to elect qualified boards of directors who would improve corporate performance.

The task force emphasized that pension funds should follow a voice model. Under this model, when performance lags, the investor's response should be to speak up if invested in an index fund, and not to exit if invested directly in individual corporations. In sum, the generic components of the voice model were the duty to communicate, the duty to participate in corporate governance, and the duty to be accountable. By using their voice as shareholders, pension funds could show their support, visibly, for the longer-term balanced performance we urged for corporations. *Our Money's Worth* modeled pension-fund governance and facilitated the government and companies working together to find common ground, much in line with the objective of the Institutional Investor Project.

THE WORKING GROUP ON CORPORATE GOVERNANCE: TREETOPS AND ROOTS

The Institutional Investor Project and The New York State Task Force on Pension Fund Investment were steps toward bringing together institutional investors, directors, and management. Yet, in the early 1990s, even though there was a slowdown in hostile takeovers and LBOs, the division between shareholder rights, on the one hand, and director powers, on the other, continued to stir debate in public and private forums. There was growing concern about the appropriate roles and responsibilities of shareholders and directors. How can a company balance shareholder needs with corporate performance in the short term? It was quite clear to many of us that shareholders and directors needed more guidance on their responsibilities if we were to ease the existing tensions over the governance of public companies.

I participated in working groups that addressed the escalating tension between institutional investors and directors. I attended meetings in 1989 and 1990 with corporate participants from General Mills, Texaco, Champion International and public pension fund participants from CalPERS, Connecticut Retirement and Trust Funds Office of the Treasurer, Massachusetts Pension Reserves Investment Management Board, New York City Office of the Comptroller, and State of Wisconsin Investment Board, among others. At these meetings we tried to untangle the complex relationships between the owners and managers of public corporations. Referred to as the "Treetops Meetings" because they were held on property owned by Champion International called Treetops, we delved into issues like the importance of communication between investors and directors, how to effectively engage in that discussion, the roles and responsibilities of boards of directors, and how corporate performance should be measured. The corporate and the pension fund participants could talk frankly about their expectations of each other and about how to build stronger relationships.

Also in 1989, I joined a working group of seven other lawyers representing large public companies and leading institutional investors called the Working Group on Corporate Governance, better known as "Roots." We called our group Roots because we believed that if we firmly planted sound corporate governance principles, corporations would flourish. It was significant that the coalition of lawyers in the working group represented two key constituencies: large public corporations and leading institutional investors.

We held a series of meetings to establish principles that reconciled the tensions between those who owned the corporation and those who managed the corporation. In 1991, after much discussion among us, we published *A New Compact for Owners and Directors*. It outlined certain principles for directors and shareholders to help each of them understand what their roles and responsibilities should be.

We recommended, for example, that the board's outside directors should routinely evaluate the performance of the CEO against established goals and strategies and should meet alone, at least once a year, coordinated by a leader. We also recommended that the directors should establish appropriate qualifications for board members and should clearly communicate those qualifications to shareholders; and that outside directors should screen and recommend candidates based on qualifications established by the board. At this point, none of these recommendations were best practice at corporations, especially the practice of outside directors meeting alone without the CEO.

The *Compact* was widely received and deemed a major contribution to the ongoing debate of public corporation governance. To me, it provided a much-needed tool for lawyers to assist corporations to develop effective corporate governance systems.

The pre-1990 work I engaged in, starting with the BRT efforts in 1978, provided me with intellectual grounding, and more important, with hands-on learning from peer groups drawn from the entire corporate community. With a handful of notable exceptions, at this point there was little useful material available on what directors should actually do.

The field of corporate governance was still in the very early stages of development. My learning came from dealing with people doing their jobs.

It was fortuitous that at about that same time I was given the opportunity to put it all to work in a real-time developing crisis at a major corporate icon central to the economy— General Motors.

3

REVOLT IN THE BOARDROOM

The Story of General Motors

This chapter tells the previously untold story of how GM directors finally woke up twenty-five years ago to deal with the company's financial meltdown. For far too long, a passive board stood by, failing to challenge management, as its seemingly untouchable executives brought GM to the brink of financial disaster. It was a watershed in the history of corporate governance that received wide coverage in the press at the time. There are very few of us left who were there. There should be a record of the work of a few courageous directors who left the fold and set the course for future corporate governance. For the first time, independent directors, meeting separately, challenged an angry, typically imperial CEO—and later fired his chosen successor publicly. I hope that their courage is ingrained in today's boardrooms to meet the demands of today's infinite variety of shareholders. The lessons learned back then are just as relevant today.

BOARD TRANSFORMATION

The Detroit hotel's meeting room was unexceptional, even for a Ritz-Carlton. The lighting was bright and harsh, the hotel furniture was reproduction "antiques." There were no microphones, no podium. Ballpoint pens and notepads with the hotel's logo were at each seat, a pitcher of ice water and glasses on the table. The room was too cold.

The setting was classically ordinary, even boring. I sat around the table in 1992 with the outside directors of General Motors Corp., people of standing and experience in their respective fields, who had *never* before assembled without someone from management present. Only a decade earlier, GM was the world's largest and most powerful auto company. Its massive headquarters on West Grand Boulevard dominated downtown Detroit.

The remarkable Albert Khan–designed neoclassic structure, topped by a two-story Corinthian colonnade, has four parallel fifteen-story wings connected to a central perpendicular backbone and is served by thirty-one elevators. Faced in limestone, the building's entrance has Italian marble walls and gray Tennessee marble floors, giving the impression of intimidating power, stability, and permanence.

Unfortunately, the reality of GM at the time had none of those qualities. Its market share was in free fall, dropping to 35 percent from 45 percent in only ten years beginning in 1980. Once Detroit's lowest-cost automaker, it was now its highest. Its core North American unit was losing money. The look-alike cars the division produced were of poor quality. It was hard to tell which nameplate was which. GM was caught in the trap of huge structural costs—in 1984 the company had granted union demands for a contract that included a provision that workers would be paid even if they were laid off.

With a cost structure that exceeds revenue, one financial crisis will surely follow another, forcing asset sales or new debt. GM did not trim itself by taking out the people it should have taken out. It did not close plants it should have closed. It did not aggressively reduce long-term benefits packages that were noncompetitive against the Japanese and produced a cost differential of up to $1,500 a car. Obviously, GM needed to make difficult choices to be competitive.

Roger Smith, CEO and chairman of the board of directors, was not a "car guy," in Detroit terminology, but rather a finance guy who joined GM in 1949 as an accounting clerk. He ruled "his" board autocratically. The highly formalistic meetings, held in an imposing dark-paneled GM boardroom lined with portraits of former CEOs and chairmen, seemed to anesthetize directors, not inform them. Carefully orchestrated, the "good news" presentations of slides and charts focused on matters such as how well certain brands—like Chevrolet—were selling, never mentioning the ones that weren't doing very well, like Oldsmobile or Cadillac. As managers droned on, directors could follow along word-for-word with a loose-leaf briefing book. These presentations mostly provided details irrelevant to competition and declining sales. Managers had a second briefing book that included relevant information and numbers to refer to if directors questioned anything, but that was rare, in my experience. Should anyone even approach the topic of management performance, Roger would quickly change the subject, cutting off any chance of meaningful discussion.

Roger was self-confident, despite GM's decline, and even though he had some of the top CEOs in the country sitting around the table, he didn't want to draw them out or extract their knowledge. I sensed that he didn't care if it was the CEO of Merck or P&G. In his opinion, General Motors did things differently, and everyone should just go along. No one became a board member who was not blessed by Roger.

Roger handpicked the members of the finance committee, arguably the board's most important group. It was a sort of mini-board, through which everything was funneled. Many directors who weren't on it told me they felt they were second-tier.

Roger, of course, chaired the committee. The only thing the full board would get was a committee report—very different from experiencing the three- or four-hour deliberation the committee might have over key issues. It was another example of Roger's total control. Some of the directors complained to me they didn't have what they needed to do their jobs.

It was a similar scene in many U.S. boardrooms at the time. This was the era of the imperial CEO. The imperial CEO generally left directors, and certainly shareholders, largely uninformed about what was really happening, especially when things weren't going well for the company. To a remarkable extent, both groups were content to go along. Director fees were not excessive, nor the reason for joining the GM board. Rather, it was a mark of status, the honor of directing the biggest car company in the world. To be a director of GM meant you had arrived in corporate America. Roger's behavior was not uncharacteristic for the times. Shareholders were generally passive. They hadn't yet found their voices.

It was common practice for CEOs in those days to recruit directors who were there to support them, period. Directors weren't there to pick fights. Directors could ask questions and so on, but they hadn't been picked by shareholders, or through any kind of shareholder referendum—they had been picked by the CEO, and, perhaps, by a few like-minded directors. Some were well-known public figures, such as Washington, DC, attorney Vernon Jordan Jr., who was brilliant, well connected, and respected. These stars were ubiquitous and praised in the press for juggling so many balls at the same time. In his career, Vernon has served on the boards of American Express, J. C. Penney, Dow Jones, Revlon, Sara Lee, Corning, Xerox, and RJR Nabisco during the 1989 leveraged buyout fight with Henry Kravis's KKR.

I thought directors who served on multiple boards were not what a company needed. How many hours were in their days? How could they be diligent, well-informed board members, steeped in the company's business? When asked, I always tell people who want to serve on a board because it would "look good on their resumes," not to do it. Why? Because it's no fun unless you care about the business and participate by doing your homework, attending meetings, and asking questions.

My involvement with GM board matters began shortly after a 1985 lunch meeting with Elmer Johnson, then the GM general counsel. We had known each other from

Weil's previous success in defending GM in a shareholder suit involving alleged brake defects in certain vehicles. The topic of the lunch discussion was the oversight of two new classes of stock (E and H) issued in conjunction with the acquisitions of Electronic Data Systems (EDS) and Hughes Aircraft. We decided that the board probably needed some kind of committee to deal with governance and potential litigation issues related to the new classes, which I believed could constitute fertile proving grounds for new legal theories.

The board agreed and formed the Common Stock Classification Oversight Subcommittee of the Audit Committee, which subsequently was made a standing board committee, for which I served as counsel. That involvement and my informal advising of individual outside directors on various matters soon led to the outside directors retaining me as their legal counsel.

That was a time when many outside directors in America's leading boardrooms were not only kept in the dark, but were hamstrung by the long-established ban on meeting with each other separately outside the boardroom. Maybe men's room chats and telephone calls were acceptable, but not formal meetings without management present. That was just the way it was. Meeting without management was treason. Many directors told me at the time that their job was to "support" the CEO, not question critically or meet with other directors without management present.

One day I had lunch at the Plaza Hotel across the street from the GM building in Manhattan with Ellmore Patterson, chairman and CEO of J.P. Morgan. I wasn't back in my office for more than a minute before Roger Smith barged in. At that time, GM occupied most of the office space in the GM building. Roger insisted on knowing what I was doing having an "unauthorized" meeting with a company director.

"We were discussing New York City's fiscal crisis," was my honest answer. "Besides, I'm counsel to the board, and I can meet with a director if he or she asks."

"No, you can't," said Roger. "You're not to meet with my directors alone!" Then he stormed out, red faced. That's how it was, and I was on a tightrope doing my job.

Through rumors, press scrutiny of the company's growing troubles, and other adverse publicity, the outside GM directors soon realized just how much they didn't know. *The Wall Street Journal,* for example, dug up a customer who was very unhappy with an '82 Chevrolet Citation. Its power steering was sluggish and hard to turn during the first ten to fifteen minutes of driving. It turned out that GM had identified the problem in 600,000 cars built between 1982 and 1988, even giving it a name: "morning sickness." GM quietly extended warranty coverage on the power steering units and offered free repairs to buyers who complained, but there was no public acknowledgment of the defect. The unhappy customer bought an '89 Toyota Camry, and said under no circumstances would he ever buy a GM car again. "I really don't trust them," he told the paper.

This was another symptom either ignored or buried. As the World War II years faded, Japan and Germany regained industrial strength, virtually starting from scratch with help from the United States. Their vehicles became more than simply competitive. They were better. And GM for a long while refused to recognize how the industrial world was changing.

Not helping GM's image was *Roger & Me*, a wickedly unflattering and misleading documentary by rogue film-maker Michael Moore, the son of a GM worker. The movie portrayed Roger as the evil, coldhearted destroyer of Flint, Michigan, where the company had laid off thousands of workers. The 1989 film came at precisely the wrong time for GM.

Directors were increasingly aware, concerned, and fed up with Roger's controlling, dismissive attitude. Then Roger received a letter from Dale Hanson, who headed the giant California Public Employees' Retirement System (CalPERS) pension fund, a big investor in GM. The letter expressed concerns about the company's poor performance. Dale wanted a meeting. Without consulting the board, Roger brushed off CalPERS, refusing to meet with him. Dale told me that Roger later relented and there was a cold, unproductive meeting with CalPERS, for which Roger had no respect.

Growing especially concerned was John Smale, a GM director and chairman of Procter & Gamble, one of the best-run consumer-focused companies in America. He was upset about the rose-tinted news the board received. The deteriorating market share numbers and the troubled North American division's profitability were never discussed. If any-one asked how GM's profitability matched up against, say, Ford's, the answer would always be something like "we'll get back to you," and a response often took months. The company was close to $130 billion in revenue and should have been making more than the paltry $4.2 billion it earned in 1989.

Over the next three years losses totaled $30 billion. The board understood that. John and I repeatedly talked about the problem and agreed that the outside directors simply had to be better informed.

To his credit, Roger tried to turn things around. His strategies just never worked very well. In 1984, he bought EDS for $2.5 billion. EDS was the big database outfit run by Ross Perot, the prickly, opinionated executive who brought his own set of problems to the table. Ross joined the GM board as part of the deal, but his style and impatience clashed with Roger's style, and also often with that of the other directors. Their relationship ruptured openly in September 1985, during a meeting in Dallas over EDS executive compensation. Roger was reluctant to accept the EDS plan and substituted one of his own, which an EDS financial official during the meeting called "inferior." Roger was enraged. Doron Levin's book *Irreconcilable Differences* (1989) describes the aftermath:

> People in the room later would remember Smith's angry explosion as being wondrous and terrifying at the same time: wondrous for the extreme colors and sounds it brought to the room, terrifying because none of them had ever seen someone lose his temper so completely in a business meeting. The EDS officers stared in disbelief as the chairman of the world's biggest and most powerful company lost it.

The concept behind the EDS deal was to revamp GM's communication and computer systems. But EDS had no experience in manufacturing, so GM had to spend an enormous amount of time and money teaching them how to do all of this. EDS was spun off in 1995. It was a bitter end to a failed marriage—but it placated GM's shareholders, at least in the short term, by delivering value to them that they couldn't get from owning GM.

Just so, the 1985 $5.2 billion purchase of Hughes Aircraft sounded like a good idea at the time. GM was supposed to take Hughes's aerospace systems engineering expertise and apply it to the car-making business. But what it really did was add cost and complexity to vehicle development without any of the hoped-for efficiencies. Why? Because making a car is not like making a rocket.

The bottom line was this: these two acquisitions were very, very costly for GM. In hindsight, it is clear that GM would have been far better to take all those billions of dollars, pay down its long-term debt, put the balance sheet in a stronger position, and pay more attention to quality. But that wasn't done. (To be fair, it wasn't done in the rest of the U.S. auto industry either.)

Then there was automation. Roger wanted to modernize GM using advanced technologies, envisioning "lights out" factories where the only employees were supervisors to run the computers and robots—a concept not terribly popular with the United Automobile Workers labor union. Roger spent tens of millions of dollars on robots, some of which, it was reported to me, wound up painting each other and welding car doors shut. GM removed several of the robots from some plants shortly after they were installed. Responding to a 1986 report on three-year capital expenditures

REVOLT IN THE BOARDROOM

projected at almost $35 billion, Vice President of Finance F. Alan Smith (no relation to Roger) posited that money could have been better spent on buying both Toyota and Nissan, which would have bumped up their market share overnight arguably much higher than the planned internal investment. He was ignored.

The technology effort followed Roger's equally ill-fated 1984 reorganization, where he sought to streamline the company by creating three units—one for big cars, one for small cars, and one for trucks. But the efficiencies never emerged. To the contrary, the plan added costs and created new bureaucracies, duplicating existing positions at the corporate and division levels. The move had precisely the opposite effect of its intention and was ultimately abandoned, albeit not for ten years. Car buyers yawned at the new line of midsized cars introduced in 1988 by Chevrolet, Oldsmobile, Pontiac, and Buick. The similar-looking models were plagued by cost, quality, and safety concerns.

Perhaps even more alarming was the conversation Roger had one day over lunch with his in-house counsel, Harry Pearce. "Harry, you know, it really doesn't matter what GM makes. We could be making widgets. All that matters is that we make money." Harry was dumbfounded. Here was the head of the world's largest car company telling his general counsel that all he cared about was the numbers, not the products or their deteriorating quality.

Another Roger idea in August 1986, again oriented to money and not car quality, was what he called "the Big One"—2.9 percent financing. It was the lowest in GM's history. The market share spiked up, then once all those vehicles were sold for not much above cost, the market share plummeted.

Harry has in the past called Smith's entire plan an "ill-conceived scheme" that didn't address the underlying problem: quality control in the plants and quality design of components, systems, and overall vehicles. "We had horrendous problems, and many, many senior people at GM understood it and wanted to work on it, but that did not seem to be Roger's focus."

Smith retired in the summer of 1990, when he would turn 65. Two emboldened outside directors—John Smale and Marvin Goldberger, director of the Institute for Advanced Study in Princeton, New Jersey—had raised concerns with Roger about board procedures, including information disseminated to the board, and asked exactly how GM expected to turn the North American operations profitable by 1992, as management promised. Harry and I had sent Roger several memos during that last year, stressing the need for meaningful board involvement.

Perhaps most important, I counseled director Jim Evans, who chaired Union Pacific, about the directors' fiduciary duties, focusing on the need to show prudent oversight on key strategic issues. Jim was by then a personal friend, and he eventually turned the chairmanship of the Central Park Conservancy over to me. Courts were scrutinizing the role of outside directors in those days, including in Delaware Supreme Court cases *Smith v. Van Gorkom* and *Unocal Corp. v. Mesa Petroleum Co.* Decisions by fully informed directors who followed a process of careful deliberation leading to a considered strategy had been given near-dispositive weight.

By contrast, outside directors who were ill-informed or who took too passive a role were penalized.

So it was important for Roger to respond to director concerns. I made it clear to the directors that it was strongly advisable for them to involve themselves more, given the possibility, albeit remote, of a stockholder lawsuit.

Realizing that things were unraveling quickly, I consulted with Harry, who adamantly agreed how urgent it was to gather the outside directors, without Roger, to discuss board strategy and move forward. The plan was to book a room at the Ritz-Carlton, where all the out-of-towners stayed the night before the full board meeting. I would tell them that it was vital that they activate, as things were unraveling fast. But outside directors didn't meet alone without management, and some directors were nervous when I told them what I had in mind. They knew Roger would be furious. "So what?" I said. "You're the *directors*. You are by law in charge of the corporation, which is to be 'managed by or under the direction of the board.'" It was perfectly proper, and even necessary, but in no big U.S. corporation that I or the board members knew of, had independent directors formally met alone.

The meeting with the outside directors began uneventfully, though the directors were visibly tense and uncomfortable. What if Roger found out about the meeting? What if he found out where we were? We were just sitting there talking when the door flew open. *It was Roger.*

Somehow he'd found out about the meeting, possibly from a hotel employee. We never figured that out. But Roger was clearly upset. "This looks like a directors meeting. I'd like to join you," he said, about to take a seat.

John Smale was calm and firm. "This is a meeting of *outside* directors," he said. "We want to meet without you, Roger."

Roger turned purple, veins popping out on his neck and forehead. "You can't do that!" he said forcefully.

"Yes we can," John replied. "You're excused." Insulted that he was being instructed to leave by *his* directors, Roger slammed the door on the way out.

The tension broke. Everyone took a deep breath. It was the beginning of real corporate governance at General Motors. Independent directors coalesced to think and plan together, and talk frankly about management.

Of course Roger saw this as a vast conspiracy of the board to overthrow him, though the directors made it clear that wasn't the point at all of the meeting.

Harry recalls one senior management committee meeting where Roger was "just out of control," shouting about how he didn't "want this lawyer, this Mr. Millstein, sticking his nose into all of GM's business when he wasn't asked." Roger was furious about my involvement: *"How did Ira find out about this?"* he demanded. I found out about it because I'd been retained by the outside directors to inquire where I deemed necessary and to ask the appropriate questions. I had come to know the company and the directors well. Harry was embarrassed by the outburst. "It was a real turnoff to me because that's not the way I expect a chief executive officer to behave," he recalls.

But Roger, I believe, had respect for my judgment, and me, and I respected him. As a finance guy he tried everything, except to focus hard on the actual product—cars. Many of our one-on-one meetings and phone calls were difficult. My fallback position was always to acknowledge that I knew he was concerned that I was talking to directors, but that it was *my job*—since I was representing them at their request—to address the major issues they had told me of, and our skirmishes weren't personal.

I was lucky to have Harry. We both saw the same objective in the role of the general counsel and counsel to the board: to involve the board as much as possible—with all the relevant facts. With Roger in charge, that was not an easy task.

As the board contemplated Roger's successor, I impressed on them how important it was that their actions be thorough and considered, both procedurally and substantively—and totally defensible if any shareholder questioned the legitimacy of the process and whether the board had done its job. I pressed forward with outside directors John Smale, Jim Evans, Marvin Goldberger, and Tom Wyman, with Harry always there. By this time they were far more than clients; we were allies and friends fighting for the life of the company. We spoke regularly about their aspirations and objectives: Did the board identify the key challenges facing the company and relate those challenges to the qualities it sought in a new CEO? What information about the company, the industry, and the candidates did it seek in its deliberations? What were the expectations of the new CEO? What were the new CEO's expectations in dealing with the board? Procedurally, how did the board go about answering those questions? What was done by the full board? What was done by the committees? Who did the board and committees turn to for advice and information? What was delegated to experts within or outside the company? What was delegated to management?

Following these guidelines, the board fairly quickly focused on Robert (Bob) Stempel, 57, a true "car guy" who joined GM in 1958 in the Oldsmobile design department. He was named an executive vice president and a director in 1986, and then president and COO the following year. A mechanical engineer by training, Bob helped pay his way through college working as a mechanic, fixing his fellow students' cars. Big (6′ 4″) and personable with a booming voice, Bob was an imposing figure who quickly gained the trust and admiration of not only his fellow executives but also the men on the factory floor.

Bob succeeded Roger as chairman and CEO in July 1990, the day before Iraq invaded Kuwait. The invasion pushed the United States into a recession, crimping auto sales. Bob once joked to a *Reuters* reporter that he had "only one good day as chairman."

It was an exaggeration, perhaps, but not by much. The troubles that had plagued the automaker continued, and the finances were still unraveling. In less than two years it was clear that Bob was not the man to lead General Motors. He had not demonstrated to the board a strategy to save the company. This time the directors were alert, keen to act, if for nothing more than to ensure there would be a record of their active involvement in overseeing management.

Even so, not much was changing. The meaningful information Bob was sharing with the board was no different than what Smith had shared. Harry and I pleaded with Bob about the importance of an immediate impact—much like the importance of a new U.S. president's first 100 days. We emphasized that Bob must elicit the board's opinion, and, in both perception and reality, send out the signal that the new CEO and the board were "in synch." We pointed out that the stakes at GM were particularly high, far more so than at most other U.S. corporations. If GM stumbled, hundreds of thousands of people would suffer, and so would the U.S. economy. "The board is, as a practical matter," I said to Bob, "the sole overseer of GM's current and future performance."

Harry and I highlighted that the company needed leadership and direction at all levels. With the goodwill and high expectations of success from the entire GM family—directors, managers, employees, dealers, customers, and suppliers—I emphasized to the directors that Bob "should try to get off the mark appropriately so as to meet those expectations. I don't think it is an overstatement to say that a great corporation, and all the people who depend on it, will be significantly impacted by how Bob Stempel starts."

I circulated these thoughts to our coterie of outside directors—Smale, Evans, Goldberger, and Wyman. They enthusiastically supported the urgency and goals. Most planned to leverage the ideas to stimulate their own one-on-one meetings with Bob, which were to begin immediately. Tom Wyman, among the first to sit down with Bob, said he intended to highlight the 100-day model, the high expectations everyone held, the board's desire to help, and the board's need to "erase the blackboard"—meaning that we weren't criticizing Bob—but that whatever Bob intended to do, he should do it quickly and signal clearly to the board what his mission was.

Marvin Goldberger said he'd raise several issues with Bob, including eliminating the meeting's show-and-tell flavor. "Currently it's a scene like a third-grade reading period with the teacher calling on prize pupils," he told me. He also said he'd suggest that the board meet once a year for up to a day and a half with a relatively unstructured agenda to discuss major issues in depth. Most important, obviously referring to Roger, "it must be made unambiguously clear that we have no intention of being terrorized as in the past."

Bob moved around some desk chairs and was certainly easier to deal with. The board meetings were less formulaic. Management presenters were encouraged to distribute written memos to the board before the meeting, so that meeting time could be devoted to questions, not script-reading.

But overall strategy didn't change much at first. There was broad consensus in a series of interviews conducted in early 1991 by Harry, at John's suggestion, with the board and key midlevel officers, that GM's North American product plan was fundamentally flawed, as was the organizational structure that supported it. Harry's work was politely worded, of course, but he pulled no punches. The directors had reached uncomfortable conclusions: that Bob's stated strategy of introducing more new products than anyone else year after year was self-defeating. GM didn't even have the engineering resources for what it was trying to do currently. Harry pointed out something else: "Some of our best engineers would tell you that they are overworked and stretched so thinly that product mediocrity is almost guaranteed... They hardly have time to react to the daily demands our proliferation of product places on them."

Spreading capital so thinly among so many products wasn't helped by the widespread belief that each new GM model would be the one to solve all the problems and capture new market share. But that hope was dashed by quality and customer feedback issues. The platypus-nosed Pontiac, Oldsmobile, and Chevrolet minivans (in reality identical vehicles with only minor distinguishing touches) didn't come close to the quality and customer satisfaction of the Toyota Previa. And the four-door Blazer had twice the problems per one hundred vehicles as the beautifully styled Ford Explorer, which was a major success for Ford. For each failure or "average" introduction, GM always rationalized thus: The futuristic styling of X will take time for consumer acceptance, Y will do well as soon as we have four-door models, and so on.

GM's embedded culture, in which confrontation was to be avoided, meant that there were many executives in important positions who had proven themselves not up to the task but who were still around, seemingly impregnable. In April 1991, I shared with Tom Wyman and Jim Evans a private memo sent by Harry to Bill Marriott, another outside director. I called it the tip of an iceberg that other directors must discuss.

The memo concerned the makeup of the management committee, a group filled largely by senior executives who would never be CEO. Many of them had in fact already failed in key management positions in the North American unit, the part of the company most in trouble.

The result, according to Harry, was that GM's core business was being run by a very weak management team, compounded by the chief financial officer, Robert O'Connell. Although a decent person, O'Connell was widely viewed by others in management as ineffective, with nonexistent communication or leadership skills.

Harry recommended specific changes, including putting Jack Smith, who'd done a superb job running international operations, in charge of the troubled North American unit. Bob Eaton, a talented car executive then head of GM Europe, would succeed Jack, and Robert O'Connell would be replaced by a "first-rate" CFO and would either be offered a buyout package or given a job that would "keep him completely out of the operating side of the business." To deal with Lloyd Reuss, the head of GM North America, Harry proposed creating a second presidency to preside over EDS and Hughes, a position he said could be "portrayed as a lateral move."

It is a measure of Harry's courage as a GM executive that he sent such recommendations outside the building. It underscored his real fear that the company was heading toward insolvency. He believed the only solution was for GM to put tough-minded, decisive managers in place who would do whatever was necessary to make the North American unit profitable. "I am not at all comfortable speaking this frankly and critically about some of my fellow executives," he concluded, "but I firmly believe the financial viability of the corporation is at stake."

Picking up on this urgent tone, John suggested directly to Bob that GM embrace a more entrepreneurial model by breaking down the organization into logical "small business" units that would focus on specific consumer product segments like compacts, utility vehicles, and station wagons. Each unit would be responsible for design, quality, product engineering, manufacturing, and profit—the latter incorporating all allocated costs for staff and overhead. Was it surprising that this approach was remarkably similar to P&G's?

Meanwhile, some of Bob's moves continued to puzzle the board. Early on he had proposed devoting the main presentation of one of his first board meetings to remarks by George Eads, the well-regarded GM economist, who would speak about the global economic outlook. Reacting to criticism that the time might be better spent discussing GM's death spiral, Bob changed the agenda and inserted George in a later meeting with reduced time.

Then there was Bob's bizarre suggestion in April 1991 that the base salaries of directors, management committee members, and group executives be temporarily reduced by 10 percent, presumably to signal the company's seriousness about cost cutting. There was silence around the table when that was proposed. The problem: GM was planning a compensation restructuring in the fall, which would result in handsome base salary increases for the top-rated executives—a legitimate move to attract and retain the best people during a crisis. But once that news leaked out, as it surely would, the United Automobile Workers would likely call the 10 percent pay cut a devious and bad-faith charade, complicating GM's bargaining position in the reopening of labor contracts. Tom Wyman and John were stunned that Bob didn't see this as a possibility. The proposal was quietly shelved.

And some directors were shocked to see Roger, who was still a director—at least on paper—show up to some meetings. Marvin Goldberger said Roger's presence was "distressing" and "inhibiting," since the board was in the process of looking for "replacements for the failed policies of the past." "I can't believe Bob doesn't find it awkward as well," Goldberger added in his letter to John, who later disinvited Roger to any parts of the meetings that discussed corporate governance.

But Goldberger's main complaint, as he expressed in a letter to John in June, was the absence of any sense of real change, a realistic forward agenda, or recognition of past procedures that must be changed. "Obviously cultural changes at GM are difficult, but Bob has been in office for nine months and his gestation period has not yet produced any visible offspring and the pattern of floundering continues."

Harry met over the summer with Bob Eaton, the impressive head of GM's European operations. Eaton was a man everyone looked to. He was set for more responsibilities in the near future. Eaton told Harry what many others had been saying: under the current structure, GM did not have the design or manufacturing capacity to create a world-class car because there were no profit centers, there was too much necessary coordination, and too many committees to get good ideas off the ground. And there was no accountability anywhere. Eaton openly worried whether Bob "has the gauge to do the necessary, culturally and otherwise."

In the fall of 1991, the pace of director unease increased. Bill Marriott challenged Bob's earlier claim that GM would break even the following year. Marriott cited weak buyer demand, excess production capacity, the high cost of paying laid-off employees, and the estimated loss of $2,500 per vehicle on fleet sales, which made up 41 percent of revenues. "Bob, I'm concerned about our big outflow of cash and the possibility that it will continue with very dangerous consequences." Referring to the upcoming November board meeting, Bill said: "I assume that the outside directors will not include Roger Smith."

In December, John Smale relayed his concerns to Bob that the board was too much in the dark about the cost-reduction programs then being implemented. Referring to an earlier Washington, DC, board meeting, John said, "Time didn't provide nearly enough opportunity to get a clear understanding of both these programs." Though he didn't spell it out, that lack of understanding might be interpreted by courts as a lack of due care, which is key to the business judgment rule that protects directors who make decisions on an informed basis. If a director loses the protection of the business judgment rule, the director becomes vulnerable in litigation.

John asked for more time at the next board meeting for a detailed explanation of the cost-reduction programs, particularly how they related to Bob's assertion that the North American unit, which had lost money for the previous eight years, would suddenly be profitable. John also challenged GM's philosophy on reducing capital spending, which was to stretch out programs, not cancel them. "I worry very much about stretching out product improvement programs. It seems to me we are currently not competitive with the Japanese in relation to how long it takes us to make major changes in our product platforms. Stretching these programs out will make matters worse."

I worried about Bob's upcoming trip to Japan in January 1992 with President Bush and an entourage of other U.S. auto executives. They intended to pressure Tokyo to open its markets to American exports. The sessions promised to be contentious, but Prime Minister Kiichi Miyazawa reassured everyone by saying "even if we engage in debate, the outcome won't be war." Executives returning from such "take a firm stand" trips often come back pumped up, supported by the White House, newly confident of their own personal beliefs and policies. It was just that much more difficult for them to embrace change. Harry and I believed the directors would be intimidated.

So on December 30, 1991, I asked Bob Messineo, then a young partner at my firm, to come up with a list of things that might happen at the next board meeting that would require legal judgments. I wanted to get into the boardroom, or at the least, get Harry in there to keep things going. I wanted to get Harry's thoughts. I quickly got on the phone with Harry to "review the bidding" and see where we were. "*This is really critical*," I concluded.

Early in the new year, GM announced a staggering net loss of $4.5 billion for 1991, $2.5 billion of that in the fourth quarter alone, mostly from a $1.8 billion charge for previously announced plant closings. Sales from the hemorrhaging North American unit were down 14 percent from 1990's already depressed levels. The company also revealed the names of twelve of the twenty-one plants it planned to close, including two iconic assembly plants in Willow Run, Michigan, and North Tarrytown, New York, and an engine plant in Flint, Michigan. The closings would eliminate sixteen thousand jobs. The company said it would consolidate sales and marketing of the various auto groups into a new single unit, and would save $14 million a year by cutting benefits of former executives, including, of course, Roger Smith's.

But would these cuts be enough to salvage the disintegrating business? The board had grave doubts. Among other things, the outside directors agreed on January 5, 1992 to hold more frequent meetings alone and they appointed John Smale as a committee of one to act on their behalf to gather what information they needed to make informed decisions. This included authorizing John to spend as much time and have as much access to management as he deemed necessary for the outside directors to fulfill their responsibilities diligently and prudently. John was the logical choice for this role. He was always the one outside directors turned to when a difficult issue came up for discussion. The directors agreed that the flow of information had improved, but was still insufficient. Many of them believed that they needed more information to evaluate management's plans and capabilities as GM deteriorated. They agreed to keep these new arrangements confidential, as media reaction to it "would not be in the best interests" of GM.

Then I received a very unwelcome assignment from John on January 9. I was to bear the bad news and explain, as simply and directly as possible, the outside directors' concerns to Bob. Harry would be asked to attend as well. It was important to meet quickly since part of the plan was for John to meet one-on-one with Bob after my meeting.

I was to lay it out clearly to him: None of this was personal, but it was a special situation that required the directors' heightened interest in what was going on so they could exercise their best business judgment. John would be interviewing managers one-on-one to review programs and procedures in detail before the February board meeting to provide directors with adequate information. To that end, I would urge Bob not to resist, and to extend John total access to information and to his managers. And I would tell him that pushing back would escalate the situation and give John a further vote of confidence from the board—and against Bob.

So on January 10, I called Sylvia, Bob's secretary, and told her it was urgent that I meet with Bob as soon as possible on behalf of the outside directors. That might be difficult, she said. Bob was just now returning from Japan, had "many, many people" on his list to call, and would soon be consumed by speeches and meetings related to the auto show, which was coming up on the weekend.

I told Sylvia that I was sympathetic to his crowded schedule, but this was a matter of importance and I must see him at the earliest possible opportunity. I gave her numbers where I could be reached over the weekend and urged her to call me just as soon as she could.

Bob at first declined to meet me but gave in when Sylvia explained that John and the outside directors were behind it. On January 15, 1992, we met in a huge empty GM hangar at the Detroit airport. In the middle of the hangar were a small folding table and three folding chairs.

Harry and I sat opposite Bob and laid out our case. John asked me to give Bob an advance warning that the board was unhappy and that he'd very likely be out of a job soon.

"I don't want you to frighten him, just give him a heads-up."
I did my best.

Bob just sat there with a yellow pad, writing down every word I said. No comments, no questions. At the end, he just got up and walked out.

"Harry, what just happened?" I asked.

"Damned if I know," he said. "I've never seen anything like that."

I flew back to New York. John called.

"Did you talk to him?"

"Yes."

"What happened?"

"I have no idea. All I know is that he took copious notes."

John moved quickly with his new assignment. By mid-March, he'd produced something he called the "Red Book"—a report that was nothing short of frightening. Though the information included was all generated by GM, the directors would find it shocking—they were never told this before, and many would believe they'd been affirmatively misled over the years. I pointed out to Harry that while there were exposure and privilege issues involved, such concerns were outweighed by the need to inform the directors.

John's report read like a little horror story. He believed that quality was a problem that GM had no idea how to solve, and that to many managers, quality was an issue of perception, not reality—a scary thought indeed. The fundamental cost problem was the length of time it took to assemble a car: 37.7 hours at GM in 1991 versus 22.5 hours at Ford. There were simply basic manufacturing inefficiencies at GM. Cash flow had been a negative $22 billion in the previous seven years, including an *anticipated $4 billion* outflow in 1992. The cost of debt in 1992 would be $1.2 billion, up from $800 million in 1991. "The question obviously is how much longer we can keep this up. I'm not sure of the answer, but I suspect it's not very long."

Things were starting to get interesting. John's Red Book and notes from all of his interviews were distributed to directors' hotel rooms for an independent directors meeting on March 28, 1992, in Salon 1 of Chicago's Marriott Suites Hotel.

I added up all the Red Book conclusions, and other materials, and concluded that directors clearly *had to do something*. The goal, of course, was to exercise their best business judgment, which would mean deciding whether management had an adequate plan for the crisis and whether directors believed this particular management team could pull it off.

This particular independent directors meeting sticks in my memory. Tom Wyman and John didn't want it arranged through anyone at GM. They asked me to make the arrangements, including notifying the directors by telephone. I arranged a teleconference through my office, and since it was held at an off-hour, I participated from my living room in Mamaroneck, New York. I thought, "This is really unusual."

It was logical to assume the board would conclude that they had to act. If so, what were the options? Keep Bob? If so, doing what? If he goes, does Jack Smith automatically move up? What's the best role for John Smale?

This was hardcore corporate governance.

John made the main presentation at the meeting, outlining what he'd learned from his interviews, emphasizing the widespread belief among the company's key managers that there was a high risk of major financial distress and, possibly, bankruptcy. He also reported that most midlevel managers thought the top executives couldn't meet the challenge.

The clock ticked on. The annual stockholders meeting to elect directors was scheduled for May 22. The proxy statement would be released and mailed on April 13. In the proxy statement as prepared, the current management directors were recommended for reelection, implicitly endorsing their management process. Any significant change in the management directors after the proxy statement was released would require mailing a supplement to the statement and postponing the meeting, which would surely invite close media scrutiny.

Any change in the management just after the annual meeting would project disorganization of the board, and raise questions as to whether there were plans in place that weren't disclosed to shareholders.

Not surprisingly, the outside directors agreed in the March 22 meeting that current management had to be replaced. Lloyd Reuss must go and be held responsible for the North American unit's performance. Everyone agreed that Bob Stempel must be asked some very tough questions. Those questions came at the March 28 Chicago meeting. The directors asked Bob whether he could be or wanted to be a change-maker CEO in the mold of Jack Welch, someone who could lead the implementation of the massive changes essential to save GM.

In presenting the directors' views, John Smale made it clear that directors valued Bob's knowledge of cars, his integrity and honesty, but that those qualities weren't enough. John also noted that the GM culture Bob helped develop may prevent him from removing things that worked in the past but were now impediments. "You must ask yourself whether you are prepared to dismantle the bureaucracy we see as encasing GM and inhibiting its competitive strengths."

Bob defended his current management team, said he was working on quality and had a detailed plan to close the gap with the Japanese, asserting that his team had stabilized the "terrible" problems and were now working to improve performance across the board with a prioritized step-by-step effort that he'd be happy to discuss. He said one major cultural change was that he was closing the management committee dining room and that henceforth those executives would "eat with everyone else." That was a big relief?

Bob was excused from the meeting, and the outside directors then dissected his remarks. The consensus was that he never adequately responded to the "change-maker" challenge and that there existed a big gap between what he thought was communicated to the board and what the board heard. They decided that they should inform Bob promptly of their conclusions, and called him back from the airport, where he was ready to return to Detroit on a company plane.

Reading from a statement the board had approved, I explained to Bob the unanimous conclusions of the outside directors, that Lloyd Reuss would accept early retirement and not stand for reelection as a director; that Jack Smith would be elected president and chief operating officer, with specific responsibility for North American operations and other duties to be enumerated later; and that John Smale would be elected chairman of the executive committee of the board, with the added function of regularly communicating with management. I made clear that, at least for the time being, Bob would retain the titles of chairman and CEO, working with Jack Smith to implement necessary strategies.

Despite the titles he retained, the moves effectively stripped Bob of control over day-to-day management of the company. Jack Smith became the de facto CEO, a perception reinforced when the head of Toyota visited GM in the fall. He met with Jack Smith, not Bob. And John Smale's reinforced position simply consolidated his influence on the board. Writing on my involvement in the shakeup of General Motors' management, *The Wall Street Journal* called me a "snake in the grass" (figure 3.1). I wasn't hurt. In fact, I loved it—it meant I was doing my job.

This wasn't all that GM introduced to corporate governance. GM's executive committee also decided to limit attendance at its sessions to outside, nonaffiliated directors when corporate governance issues were discussed. This allowed full and frank discussion without the participation of executives who had personal stakes in the discussion (figures 3.2 and 3.3).

It was around that time that John and I discussed the benefits and challenges of splitting the roles of board chairman and CEO. Though common in Europe, the concept didn't

Eminence Grise

Behind Revolt at GM, Lawyer Ira Millstein Helped Call the Shots

As Outside Directors' Adviser, He Counseled the Board To Exert Greater Control

Power Play at Secret Meeting

By JOSEPH B. WHITE
And PAUL INGRASSIA
Staff Reporters of THE WALL STREET JOURNAL

DETROIT—On Saturday, March 28, the outside directors of General Motors Corp. summoned Chairman Robert C. Stempel for a secret meeting near O'Hare Airport in Chicago. They told Mr. Stempel he wasn't moving fast enough to cure GM's ills, and then dictated their terms.

They wanted Mr. Stempel to dump two senior executives, including his longtime friend, GM President Lloyd E. Reuss. The outsiders also wanted Mr. Stempel to step down as chairman of GM's executive committee in favor of someone from their ranks, John G. Smale.

For Mr. Stempel, the meeting was a painful rebuke: He became the first GM chief executive in more than 70 years to lose control of his board. For another man in the room, New York attorney Ira M. Millstein, the meeting was a sweet and spectacular triumph in the way companies are run.

For if Mr. Smale was the leader of GM's board-room revolt, Mr. Millstein, the chief counsel to GM's outside directors for more than five years, was its ideologist. "In their permissive and passive stances, most boards are likely not to appraise the performance of CEOs critically enough . . . and to wait too long to respond to ongoing political, social and economic change," Mr. Millstein and a colleague wrote in 1988.

Few philosophers in the arena of corporate governance ever get a chance to translate their theories into practice. Mr. Millstein, however, has just done it with the largest industrial corporation in the world, which means his theories are reverberating in board rooms everywhere.

And Mr. Millstein, who has never been a GM employee or director, has done it all behind the scenes, without attracting so much as a footnote of public attention. The spotlight has been focused instead on GM's newly assertive outside directors, notably Mr. Smale, the retired chairman of Procter & Gamble Co. But, declares one GM executive angry with last week's turn of events. "Millstein is the snake in the grass on this."

Avid Audience

Not that Mr. Millstein is exactly unknown. He's a high-profile New York lawyer whose career has included teaching at Columbia University and negotiating the recent Drexel Burnham Lambert bankruptcy settlement.

But starting in 1985, Mr. Millstein has developed an increasingly close relationship with GM's outside directors. He has served as the GM board's counselor, handholder and chief adviser on corporate governance. The gregarious New York City native found fertile ground for his views as GM's once-sleepy board began to wrestle with its role in the historic decline of America's pre-eminent corporation.

Mr. Millstein, age 65, delved deeply during the 1980s into the esoteric topic of how companies are run. He is the author or co-author of two books, and dozens of academic papers and speeches on the subject. He helped to establish, and is chairman of, the board of advisers to the Institutional Investor Project at Columbia University, a think tank for study of the role of big pension funds in corporate affairs. For many years, Mr. Millstein was an adviser on corporate governance to the Business Roundtable, the business lobbying group.

His message: Directors should be far more independent of the entrenched managements of corporations, and should exert far greater influence than in the past. "New times may require new board processes," he said in a speech at Harvard's Kennedy School of Government last year. The goal, he added, is to rebuild America's competitiveness.

Shaking the Executive Suite

Mr. Millstein declined to be interviewed for this article, as did GM directors. But others familiar with the board's deliberations, and with Mr. Millstein's role, provide a road map to a climactic meeting in Dallas on April 6 when GM's directors made history.

The stage was set a week beforehand, when the outside directors—with Mr. Mill-

stein at their side—confronted Mr. Stempel in Chicago. Mr. Reuss, who had presided over losses totaling $11.68 billion in GM's North American operations over the past two years, had to go. The directors also targeted Robert T. O'Connell, GM's chief financial officer.

A shaken Mr. Stempel returned to Detroit to figure out how to salvage some role in the company for Messrs. Reuss and O'Connell. On April 6, GM announced that its stunning shake-up was "unanimously approved by the board of directors, upon recommendation by the chairman." That statement was technically correct. But Mr. Stempel, left with little choice, had merely recommended what his board told him it wanted.

Here's how GM's board-room revolt, inspired by Mr. Millstein, evolved over several years:

Making Friends

In 1985, Ira Millstein was a well-regarded corporate lawyer and a partner in the New York law firm of Weil, Gotshal and Manges, which has its offices in the GM building in midtown Manhattan. Among other things, he was representing the French Pasteur Institute in litigation with the National Institutes of Health over which of the two organizations had first identified the AIDS virus. He had also established credentials as a corporate philosopher in a 1981 book, "The Limits of Corporate Power."

GM, however, had a more mundane matter for which it wanted Mr. Millstein's counsel. The auto maker was in the process of issuing a new class of common stock in connection with its $5 billion acquisition of Hughes Aircraft Co. The new common, called GMH, represented a dividend interest in the performance of the GM unit that included Hughes. The GMH shares were thus similar to the GME shares GM had issued to finance the purchase of Electronic Data Systems Corp. in 1984.

These so-called "alphabet stocks" essentially allowed then-GM Chairman Roger B. Smith to generate new money from investors to finance acquisitions. But they also created a potential problem: GM directors worried that holders of so-called "classic" GM common could attack the company for slighting them in favor of holders of the alphabet stocks.

GM's general counsel at the time, Elmer Johnson, told the board it needed independent advice. It's not uncommon for corporate America for boards to retain outside counsel, particularly in times of difficulty. GM has done it off and on for years. Now, at the suggestion of Mr. Johnson, himself an avid student of corporate governance, the board hired Mr. Millstein.

Mr. Millstein's introduction to the GM

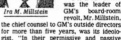

Ira M. Millstein

Figure 3.1   Ira Millstein referred to as a "snake in the grass" for his role at General Motors (1992).

board came just as the giant auto maker's fortunes were teetering. In less than two years, beginning in 1984, Mr. Smith had transformed the stodgy auto giant, completely recasting its corporate hierarchy. GM was no longer just America's No. 1 car maker. It was the nation's No. 1 computer services company, through EDS, and one of the nation's largest defense contractors, through Hughes.

But underneath all these mega-moves, GM's costs were soaring, and its quality plunging. What's more, Chairman Smith was beginning his blood feud with GM director H. Ross Perot, the Texas billionaire from whom he had purchased EDS. After weeks of negotiations, GM agreed to pay Mr. Perot $700 million for his stock, in return for his departure from the board.

Getting Advice

On Nov. 30, 1986, jittery GM directors met to approve the deal. They knew that no matter what they did, they were likely to face lawsuits from angry shareholders. They knew they needed a lawyer. They turned to Mr. Millstein.

Mr. Millstein led the GM board through carefully orchestrated deliberations that lasted some six hours. His performance sowed the seeds of what was to come.

For indeed, GM's outside directors did get sued over the Perot buy-out. And once again, they turned to Mr. Millstein. He spent hours during the months following the buy-out accompanying the directors to depositions, often having lunch with them between sessions or dinner afterward. He developed close relationships with such directors as Mr. Smale, Thomas H. Wyman, the former CBS chairman who himself was ousted in a board-room coup, and Anne L. Armstrong, a prominent Texan and former ambassador to England.

All the while, GM's fortunes were spiraling downward. In 1987, the company's share of U.S. car sales plunged to 36.3%, down nearly 10 percentage points from earlier in the decade. Mr. Smith and GM's board were coming under withering attack from big shareholders and the Perot buy-out and the company's disappointing performance. Mr. Perot, himself, derided the GM directors as "pet rocks."

A Better Idea

Against this background, Mr. Millstein in April 1987 delivered a speech to a group of big institutional investors. Investors, Mr. Millstein said, were wasting their time nitpicking corporations over such issues as anti-takeover defenses and proxy voting rules. If a company isn't performing, he said, go after the board of directors.

The message struck a nerve with some big investors, notably officials of Calpers, the $41 billion California Public Employee's Retirement System which holds a block of GM shares. "We said, 'That makes sense,' " recalls Richard Koppes, Calpers general counsel.

Mr. Millstein, in speeches and essays, began to expand on his ideas about the proper roles of big investors and outside directors. The huge pension funds, he argued, had to act as "responsible owners,"

not just short-term players in a company's stock. That meant they should put pressure on directors—their representatives—when a company isn't performing.

Directors, in turn, had to become bolder. Mr. Millstein joined a growing chorus in favor of separating leadership of the board from the position of chief executive officer. He said independent directors should meet regularly, without management, to discuss whether the chief executive measured up to the board's goals.

That hadn't happened at GM in modern memory. Mr. Millstein went further and said directors shouldn't hesitate to dismiss a chief executive who didn't perform.

The Board Stirs

Mr. Millstein, of course, also had other irons in the fire during the 1988 to 1992 period. He represented Drexel as it tottered into bankruptcy and AMR Corp., the parent of American Airlines, in an antitrust action. He served on a task force appointed by New York Gov. Mario Cuomo to study pension-fund investments.

But back at GM, the directors were stirring. Messrs. Smale and Wyman and Mrs. Armstrong, along with other outside directors, began to worry that GM's continuing malaise would start to damage their personal reputations, according to people close to the board.

In mid-1988, the outside directors jolted Chairman Smith by refusing to support his plan to put three more GM executives on the board. It was the first time Mr. Smith had been rebuffed in such a direct way. It was also a move straight out of the Millstein playbook: Mr. Millstein had been advocating that boards reduce the number of insiders.

Also, two new outside directors joined the board. One was hotel magnate J. Willard Marriott Jr., who joined in 1989, and the other Ann D. McLaughlin, former U.S. Secretary of Labor and now a visiting fellow at the Urban Institute, in 1990. Both were willing to speak their minds.

Mr. Marriott, GM insiders say, began demanding detailed information about GM's ailing North American operations. His questions encouraged Mr. Smale, who for several years had been asking why GM was earning less money than Ford Motor Co., a company just two-thirds as large. Mr. Wyman and J.P. Morgan & Co. Chairman Dennis Weatherstone—both of whom joined the board in the mid-1980s—also liked the board's new assertiveness.

In early 1990, it was time to select a successor to Chairman Smith. The obvious choice was Mr. Stempel, GM's president and chief operating officer since 1987. A reformer and conciliator instead of a revolutionary, Mr. Stempel would be the first non-finance man to head GM in more than 30 years.

But a test of wills developed over who would succeed Mr. Stempel as No. 2. Mr. Stempel wanted Mr. Reuss, a fellow engineer. The two men had worked together closely during their 32 years at GM. And after Mr. Stempel had beaten Mr. Reuss for the presidency in 1987, Mr. Reuss had

displayed tireless effort in running GM's North American vehicle operations, and in showing loyalty to Mr. Stempel.

The board balked. GM's North American operations, which Mr. Reuss was running, were losing money. The board's candidate for president was John F. "Jack" Smith Jr. (no relation to Roger Smith), who had made GM's European operations hugely profitable.

Finally the board caved in and made Mr. Reuss president, but signaled its reservations by refusing to name him chief operating officer. (Jack Smith became vice chairman for international operations.) The board was sending a message, but Mr. Stempel didn't seem to get it.

Mr. Stempel took over as chairman on Aug. 1, 1990. The next day, Iraq invaded Kuwait, and the U.S. economy plunged into a recession. GM began a "kamikaze dive," as Mr. Stempel would describe it later. GM took a $2.1 billion write-off in the third quarter of 1990 to close excess plants; its losses started to mount at a staggering rate. So did the board's impatience.

Between June 1990 and September 1991, GM rolled up five straight quarterly losses totaling $5.8 billion. Late last year, the company's outside directors began stepping up their discussions with Mr. Millstein, as did big institutional investors, such as the California Pension Fund.

Mr. Millstein became both go-between and catalyst. He assured big investors that the board was asserting itself. And he told outside directors that the investment community wanted prompt action.

Catching Up

At a board meeting on Dec. 9, Mr. Stempel said GM was working on a plan to close more factories, dismiss thousands of employees and take another huge write-off. He said the specifics weren't yet in place, but he would bring the board more details at its January meeting.

It was a huge mistake. Wall Street wanted a clear signal that GM would act promptly and decisively to stop its hemorrhaging, but Mr. Stempel was taking a deliberate tack. Securities analysts and institutional investors aired their complaints to reporters, and the company's stock dropped to a four-year low.

So on Dec. 18, Mr. Stempel hastily convened a press conference at GM headquarters. There he dropped the bombshell that GM would close 21 more plants and shed 74,000 jobs by the mid-1990s, bringing the number of factories and employees to just half their level of the mid-1980s. Internally, Mr. Stempel began telling subordinates GM must strive to break even in 1992.

To outside directors, Mr. Stempel's abrupt decision to accelerate the announcement was jarring. And the goal of breaking even just didn't sit well. They wanted the world's largest auto maker to set its sights on getting profitable, no matter what it took.

In January 1992, GM's board held its regular monthly meeting in Detroit. But Mr. Stempel was in Tokyo, reluctantly accompanying President Bush on his trade mission. The outside directors used his ab-

Figure 3.1 Continued

sence to meet privately with Mr. Millstein, a once-unthinkable act, and key board members flew back to New York with Mr. Millstein on a GM plane. Word of the huddle spread among GM executives.

The Coup

Out in California, Calpers was taking to heart Mr. Millstein's theories. The fund had written a letter to GM's board in 1990, expressing concern about the company's performance. In 1991, Calpers officials had met with Mr. Stempel to reiterate their dismay. By early this year, the fund was about to demand another meeting. But Calpers officials began getting signals from Mr. Millstein to hold off. Something was about to happen, he hinted.

Mr. Smale, at the board's behest, had begun conducting private interviews with GM's top 20 or so executives. He wanted to know what the hangups to progress were, and who was causing them. He took names, GM executives say.

In their meetings with Mr. Millstein earlier this year, the outside directors focused their views. Mr. Stempel hadn't moved fast enough last year for a company in crisis. They had completely lost confidence in Mr. Reuss, who had devised "26 strategies" for a North American turnaround that weren't producing results. And Mr. O'Connell, at least in the minds of directors, was too linked to former GM Chairman Smith, his one-time mentor.

Mr. Stempel, meanwhile, was busy damping suggestions that an executive shake-up was in the works. "Lloyd's my man," he told reporters on Feb. 24, in response to speculation that Mr. Reuss might be dumped. On March 11, in a newspaper interview, he added: "You've just got to have the patience to stay with me."

Running Out of Time

But the board's patience was nearly spent. And GM's directors were about to witness a dramatic—though entirely coincidental—example of board-room assertiveness at Chrysler Corp.: On March 16, Chrysler's board had a special Saturday meeting in New York. They rebuffed Chairman Lee A. Iacocca's bid to stay on the job beyond his retirement date at the end of this year. Chrysler's board chose Robert J. Eaton, the highly regarded head of GM Europe, to succeed Mr. Iacocca.

Two weeks later, on March 28, GM's

outside directors held their own Saturday session, in Chicago, to stand up to their chairman. With Mr. Millstein at their side, they dictated to Mr. Stempel much of the script for the events nine days later.

On Sunday afternoon, April 5, the directors flew into Dallas, home of the EDS computer-services subsidiary for their regular monthly meeting the next day. First, though, the outside directors met among themselves, with Messrs. Stempel and Millstein present. (Roger Smith, the retired GM chairman who remains on the board, wasn't invited.) At that gathering, Mr. Stempel agreed to replace Mr. Reuss as president with Jack Smith, who was already a board member. Mr. Smith also would get the title of chief operating officer, previously denied to Mr. Reuss.

But left unresolved were some key issues: Mr. Reuss's new position, and whether Mr. O'Connell would be removed as chief financial officer.

The Decision Is Made

Later, the outside directors held another private session at which Mr. Stempel addressed those issues. The final details were hashed out the next morning. All that remained was the formal vote of the full board after lunch.

Mr. Reuss, 55, was demoted to executive vice president. His duties would include a grab-bag of operations, ranging from the Saturn subsidiary to electric cars. He also was removed from GM's board, as was executive Vice President F. Alan Smith, who wasn't highly regarded by the board. The moves reduced the number of active GM executives on the board to just three of 15: Mr. Stempel, Jack Smith and Robert J. Schultz, vice chairman.

Mr. O'Connell, 53, previously an executive vice president, was demoted to senior vice president. He will take charge of General Motors Acceptance Corp., GM's big finance subsidiary.

Mr. O'Connell was replaced as chief financial officer by William E. Hoglund, 57, whose appointment was a resurrection of sorts. A GM blue-blood whose father and brother both were company vice presidents, Mr. Hoglund had long been on cool terms with Mr. Stempel. Previously in charge of components operations, he was the only one of GM's top six officers who didn't report directly to the chairman.

As for Mr. Smale, age 64, his role as

chairman of the executive committee looks remarkably like that of lead director, as described in Mr. Millstein's writings.

The Aftermath

GM announced all its moves last Monday barely 15 minutes after the board meeting broke up. The next night, April 7, Messrs. Reuss and O'Connell attended an Engineering Society of Detroit dinner at which Mr. Reuss was being honored. Even their detractors gave both men credit for making a graceful public appearance.

Mr. Reuss, besieged by reporters, said he was "disappointed but not humiliated," and pledged to stay at GM. Mr. O'Connell, for his part, quipped "27 down, 11 to go," referring to his years of service at the company, and his years until retirement.

Roger Smith, GM's former chairman, reacted stoically to the revolt by the board he had once run with an iron hand. Mr. Smith told friends that the board "just got impatient," and acted just as the company's fortunes were about to improve. Had the directors held off six months, he added, they might not have acted at all.

As for Mr. Stempel, there's widespread skepticism in the business community that he can remain an effective chairman after having his wings clipped so publicly. Last Wednesday, two days after the shake-up, Mr. Smale issued a statement saying Mr. Stempel has the board's full confidence. Directors have confided to friends that they really do hope he can make it.

"Bob's heart is in the right place," one outside director said nearly a year ago, "but bold moves aren't in his nature. He needs to be prodded. That's where the board comes in."

Mr. Millstein, for his part, was exhilarated at what happened. A friend who called him the next day found him "almost giddy" with excitement.

For finally, his ideas had come in from the cold. "We know of no case where an American corporation has been made less competitive over the long run because its board of directors was playing too active a role," he and a colleague once wrote. "We know of many whose competitiveness has deteriorated, at least in part, because boards have been too passive, and did not challenge management to see what was coming and to act before the crisis occurred."

Figure 3.1 Continued

Figure 3.2   Ira Millstein with Jack Smith (1993).

Figure 3.3   Harry Pearce, Ira Millstein, and John Smale (1996).

have wide support in the United States. Less than a dozen major companies, including Shell, Campbell Soup, and Kansas City Southern, had a nonmanagement chairman.

The conventional academic thought at the time said that an outsider might not be engaged with the dynamics of major corporate issues as they evolved, and may need a small staff on the ground to be his arms and legs within the company. I felt that this depended on the company and might or might not be an issue.

I believed that three or four full days a month carved out for regular meetings with the CEO, the CFO, general counsel, and chief auditor would keep the chairman up to speed. It was something to keep on the table as events unfolded. Bob's role was evidently redundant, Jack and John were proactive, and there was nothing for Bob to do.

So by the fall of 1992, it wasn't surprising that media speculation around Bob's exit gained traction. Both the *Los Angeles Times* and the *Washington Post* carried stories reporting that Bob had been approached to step down, reports that Bob vigorously denied. But the rumors were reinforced by a statement John issued in response to management pressure to say something. It was hardly a ringing endorsement:

> The GM board of directors has taken no action regarding any management changes at GM. However the question of executive leadership is a primary concern to the board of directors of any company and GM is no exception. The GM board of directors continues to carefully reflect upon the wisest course to take for assuring the most effective leadership for the corporation.

This even fell short of the classic "100 percent support" statement most executives or politicians make just before they open the trap door below an underperforming official.

Bob's name wasn't even mentioned. The consensus everywhere was that it was over.

But Bob didn't get it. Just a few days later, he traveled to Japan, where a *Journal* reporter asked him about the rumors. "The board has complete confidence in what I'm doing," he said. It was an incredible statement, one that sent him right into the guillotine considering our recent airport meeting. When Bob returned, John fired him on behalf of the board. Another first—a very public firing by an active board that had tried to be fair with Bob.

So on November 2, 1992 it became official. Bob was out. Not long before him, Vice President Lloyd Reuss, Vice Chairman Robert Schultz, and Executive Vice President F. Alan Smith were also replaced. Chief Financial Officer William Hoglund, the man who had earlier replaced Robert O'Connell, received a board seat but was put in charge of corporate affairs and staff support. His replacement was Rick Wagoner, a rising young executive who would later become CEO.

(Parenthetically, I was so pleased to receive a warm letter from Tom Wyman, thanking me for the advice and guidance. That was not my experience as a lawyer. My senior partner, Frank Weil, once warned me that the only place you found gratitude in the law practice was in the dictionary. I guess that fixed in my head that my group of independent directors and Harry had become far more than participants in a legal exercise—we were the best of friends in an unfolding drama starring all of us.)

Shortly after the announcement, John asked Jack and his new top managers to come in and introduce themselves to the board and make a few brief remarks. I gave them a little pep talk outside the boardroom. I told them the board was changing everything, and they were lucky to work with John and a newly activated and supported board. I told them this was the opportunity of a lifetime, and they were really going to turn things around. One by one, they went in and came out. Everyone passed muster.

Then John asked me to come in.

The directors thanked me. I was embarrassed. John asked if I wanted to say anything. I said, "Well, I wanted to congratulate all of you. You're a *real board now.*"

Everyone smiled except Ed Pratt, the chairman of Pfizer, who had been on the GM board for years. He didn't approve of what had been done, largely because it had never been done before. He was, in fact, quite unhappy with me. "We've *always* been a board," he said.

"Well, yes, but now you're doing what a board should do," I said.

Ed was unmoved. "We've *always* done the right thing," he replied.

With that, I left the room.

AN AFTERWORD

That story covers only my involvement with the GM board on governance matters over about a decade, beginning in 1985. During that time, GM, through the newly active attention of the board, became competitive again. They had lost market share dramatically in the preceding ten or more years largely due to a passive board that looked the other way as management continued to make poor decisions, to the detriment of the company and its shareholders. Much of the same board became an active board, successfully turning the ship, and created a simple model that corporate America successfully adopted. That's the lesson: a board must provide a system of checks and balances to ensure that management is accountable for its actions and acting in the best interests of the corporation. What happened in the years since is a story for others to tell as board leadership and composition changed, and I was no longer involved with the board.

In those later years competitive challenges increased from Japan, Germany, and Korea, and GM's competitive position began to erode again, to the point where bankruptcy was required to reorganize GM for the new world of global automotive preferences. I am not in a position to find fault with the new board because I wasn't close enough to know all the facts. Could the board have avoided bankruptcy, or were the legacy problems too great for GM to become globally competitive without bankruptcy reorganization? I wasn't there, I couldn't say.

4

GENERAL MOTORS AS CATALYST

The General Motors shakeup had a domino effect on corporate America. Not only did GM legitimize the concept of an active board, but soon over a dozen high-profile U.S. boards retained me to advise on board practices, including management oversight (figure 4.1). Here are some of those stories.

One of the first in the door was American Express, whose CEO, James Robinson III, was under fire from Alliance Capital and J.P. Morgan, big holders of the stock. The board wanted Robinson out, since it thought he failed to morph the firm from a credit card company into a global financial supermarket. Earnings were dropping, both at financial services (which included, at the time, Shearson Lehman) and at the flagship card unit, Travel Related Services. The whole story was told in the press later, but here is how it looked to me when I was there.

In 1991, merchants and restaurants in Boston and other cities revolted against the company's practice of "locking in" American Express as the only charge card they could

POWER BROKERS

THE GURU OF GOOD GOVERNANCE

Lawyer Ira Millstein is the éminence grise prodding companies to transform their boards

Like a caged animal, Ira M. Millstein is pacing his personal conference room at the New York law firm of Weil, Gotshal & Manges, on the 34th floor overlooking Central Park. The tall, trim 70-year-old doesn't understand why anyone would be interested in him. "Tell me," he challenges, "what's the story?"

Never mind that Millstein has been in the news a lot lately. He's advising heiress Elisabeth Goth in her campaign to prod the board of Dow Jones & Co. to do more. And as an arbitrator, he has found himself in the middle of the breakup of the four multimillionaire partners in Duty Free Shops Group.

When most lawyers his age are happiest swinging a golf club, Millstein is at the top of his professional game. An éminence grise of corporate governance, he now spends well over half his time on board issues. He teaches governance at Yale University, lectures on it to lawyers, and advises clients that include Westinghouse Electric, Estée Lauder, Empire Blue Cross & Blue Shield, and LENS, the activist investor fund.

"PET ROCK." Over nearly two decades, Millstein has helped transform the relationship between a company's board and its shareholders and management. Thanks in part to him, directors are more aware of their responsibilities, and shareholders are more likely to do something about poor performance. Along the way, Millstein has represented clients on every side of the issue: disgruntled investors, executives under attack by shareholders, and boards that want CEOs to resign.

Although he has long been a player in governance circles, it was his part in General Motors Corp.'s 1992 boardroom coup that made his name. Millstein tutored the board (once derided as "a pet rock" by departing director Ross Perot)

"STATESMAN": *He helps executives and investors find common ground*

to become more active, then guided the directors through their decision to oust Chairman and CEO Robert Stempel. GM Vice-Chairman Harry J. Pearce says Millstein "provided guidance on how to be a better company and to make sure we weren't reacting emotionally."

Remarkably, Millstein wins plaudits from people with contrasting perspectives on governance. "His role has been that of a catalyst, bringing together the institutional investors and corporate executives to get them to agree on what makes sense for everyone," notes Reginald H. Jones, former chairman of General Electric Co. Says Nell Minow, a principal of the LENS Fund: "If there is anybody in this field who could be held as a statesman, it is Ira."

With his wavy white hair, impeccably

tailored clothing, and regal bearing, Millstein looks like a statesman. Yet he speaks with boyish enthusiasm, his voice often rising to a near-falsetto as he makes a point—which usually happens behind closed doors. His professional relationships tend to broaden over time: GM's directors, for example, regard him as "a real colleague and ally," says Pearce, who talks with him "many times a week." Observers say GM seeks his input on an astonishing range of issues.

Millstein has approached his long career as a series of problems to be solved. "Torture for him would be life without a problem," laughs his wife, Diane, a real estate developer who met him when he was a teenager playing stickball on Manhattan's West 99th Street. That eagerness to grapple with thorny situations

Figure 4.1 Ira Millstein recognized as catalyst for good governance (1997).

"When General Motors went, the dominoes absolutely fell ... because GM legitimized an active board"

helped him overcome a hard-knocks upbringing. Millstein's father, a furniture salesman, prospered for a time and moved the family to suburban New Rochelle, N. Y. But he lost his house in the Depression, and the family returned to the city. Ira attended Columbia University, where he says he was told he got in "as part of the Jewish quota." To earn money, he sold hot dogs at Baker Field. He pursued a law degree after deciding that his undergraduate major, industrial engineering, was less challenging than law—and less hospitable to Jews. "Ira Millsteins," he says, "didn't get jobs in big companies in those days."

After a two-year stint as a Justice Dept. antitrust lawyer, he joined Weil Gotshal in 1951. Now a 574-attorney firm, it had only about a dozen then, and he did a bit of everything—filing tax returns, preparing wills, negotiating divorces. He graduated to antitrust, becoming one of the country's leading experts. He also became known for his fluid mind and healthy impatience.

Millstein's Vesuvian temper is infamous. His partners once insisted that his office be soundproofed. A long-running joke at the firm was that you were no one until Ira fired you—perhaps more than once. His disposition is no better away from work, says his wife, recalling the time he set a pair of tennis rackets on his car, then sped away. "He was so ticked off, he didn't play tennis for 10 years," she says. "He was mad at the tennis rackets."

"SCRAMBLERS." Millstein concedes that, early on, he was a taskmaster. "When this firm was growing up, we were scramblers," he says. "We had to read more, write more, and just win." Colleagues say Millstein, a partner since 1957, still thinks nothing of rousing them with a 6 a.m. call.

Rarely does he worry about whose ire he arouses. Last year, he chaired a National Association of Corporate Directors panel that created a key set of governance guidelines. He refused to yield on the most controversial recommendation—limiting memberships of "professional directors" to six—despite strenuous objections by panelist Ann D. McLaughlin, who sits on 16 corporate and nonprofit boards, including GM's.

Millstein's involvement in governance began when he was hired in the late 1970s as outside counsel for the Business Roundtable, the assemblage of big

company CEOs. In April, 1982, the American Law Institute drafted a report urging changes that would make it harder for courts to dismiss shareholder suits. On the Roundtable's behalf, Millstein issued a counterargument, setting off a battle with attorneys and academics. "I was attacking the temple," says Millstein, "but I was convinced down to my toenails that litigation was not the way to increase corporate performance." The Institute took until 1994 to publish its final report, but in the end, Millstein prevailed, and the section on litigation was watered down.

More important, the dispute led him to steep himself in the issue of how boards interact with management and shareholders. In 1987, he urged the new

BOARDROOM CRUSADER

BORN

Nov. 8, 1926

EDUCATION

1947 B.S. in engineering, Columbia University

1949 LL.B., Columbia University

CAREER

1949 To Justice Dept.'s Antitrust Div.

1951 Joins Weil, Gotshal & Manges

HIGHLIGHTS

1987 Urges public funds to focus efforts on boards and performance rather than social issues

1990 Helps create a board weighted with outsiders to aid the bankrupt Drexel Burnham Lambert in gaining credibility with creditors

1992 Advises General Motors board when it ousts CEO Robert Stempel

1996 Chairs National Association of Corporate Directors panel that issues broad governance guidelines

1997 Helps pressure Dow Jones board into more aggressive oversight on behalf of shareholder Elisabeth Goth

FAMILY

Married for 47 years to Diane; two children

Council of Institutional Investors to focus on performance and boards rather than poison pills and social issues. In the audience was Dale Hanson, CEO of California Public Employees' Retirement System (CalPERS). "It was a turning point," says Richard H. Koppes, then CalPERS' general counsel. "Here was a spokesman for Corporate America who said you have a legitimate gripe if you focus on performance." Within two years, the fund became a strident, often effective activist shareholder.

WATERSHED. In 1989, participants in a governance seminar began questioning Millstein about the board of client GM. "They said the board ought to be doing something," he recalls. "That led to my thinking about being more forthcoming with everybody in Detroit." Today, he divides the history of governance into "pre-GM" and "post-GM." Says Millstein: "When General Motors went, the dominoes absolutely fell. After GM, American Express, Eastman Kodak, Westinghouse, and IBM all went. They did so because GM legitimized an active board."

Millstein tends to view governance as a universal solution. Overseeing Drexel Burnham Lambert Inc.'s bankruptcy from 1990 to 1992, he won the trust of creditors by putting together a board of outsiders. He later did the same at Olympia & York Co. USA, staving off a potentially disastrous bankruptcy filing and permitting a less disruptive prepackaged bankruptcy. "Again, governance won the day," he asserts.

To help Goth pressure the board of lackluster Dow Jones, he made a list of independent directors and lobbied the company to hire them. Dow Jones added two outsiders, but not from his list. Driven by several factors—Millstein's hiring, news of Goth's campaign, and a large stake taken by hedge fund manager Michael Price—Dow Jones stock has risen 15% since late December.

Dow Jones's survival has never been at stake. It's merely a weak performer. The new challenge, says Millstein, is to squeeze better results from just such "middling, bumping-along, not-too-terrible" companies: "That would be where I would like to see boards become more active." No doubt, as that becomes the norm, Millstein will be on hand, helping to ratchet up the pressure—and advising the boards that respond.

By John A. Byrne in New York, with Keith Naughton in Detroit

Figure 4.1 Continued

accept. The tradeoff was a lower "merchant fee," but at 3.18 percent per transaction, it was still twice that of competitors like Visa and MasterCard. The Boston Fee Party became a rallying cry against American Express's perceived greed and arrogance. Spearheaded by a public relations firm reportedly hired by Discover Card, more than 250 restaurants across the United States protested American Express's business practices, with some no longer accepting American Express cards.

Then there came a messy lawsuit and a nasty smear campaign that American Express launched against Edmond Safra, a Lebanese banker who had sold his private bank to the company in 1983. In 1990 *The Wall Street Journal* published a lengthy page-one piece about the campaign, which upset Robinson and his wife, Wall Street public relations expert Linda Robinson. American Express had actually admitted and apologized for the anti-Safra campaign a year before. But the timing of the *Journal* story was odd, considering that Connie Bruck in *The New Yorker* had just sharply criticized the *Journal* for pulling its punches on Robinson in its coverage of the 1988 RJR Nabisco leveraged buyout.

In the overall scheme of things, this gossip-column chatter didn't have much effect on the company, but the snickering was an unwelcome distraction to the board. That, plus the real financial troubles and pressure from big investors, accelerated the board's conclusion that it was time for Robinson to go.

Robinson had already been talking about taking early retirement, but the board wanted a quicker exit. In September 1992, the directors and I met with Robinson in a private dining room at the St. Regis Hotel, after which he was excused. Twenty minutes later, the board asked him back and told him to come in the next morning with a plan to pick his successor. A leak to *Fortune* about the meeting and how Robinson was "compelled" to develop a succession plan forced the company to announce his departure sooner than planned.

I helped craft an arrangement that gave Robinson little more than the standard severance package for someone at his level. The settlement ignored earlier American Express precedents for early retirement that could have increased his pension significantly and added more years of pay. He reluctantly accepted the terms, which included two years of salary, a pro forma pension, an office, secretary, and use of a company car for eighteen months.

It was reported that Robinson considered the board's offer insufficient for someone who had run such a major company for sixteen years. He believed he was entitled to additional years of salary, a better pension plan, and a three-year paid consulting contract, giving him access to the corporate jet. His unusual request: he asked American Express to share in the cost of establishing a chair in his name at Harvard Business School for a course to be called "Total Quality Management." The board's answer to all these was a firm no.

At the time of Robinson's departure, Howard Clark, the retired CEO who had served as a consultant to the board after Robinson took over, told *The Wall Street Journal* that the board was "too embarrassed" to go much beyond the minimum severance package. I believe the GM saga gave boards like American Express courage to sever, on the board's terms, even a CEO of long standing and previous success when they thought it necessary. Directors in corporate America were beginning to realize that they had both the responsibility, and the authority, to more actively oversee the affairs of the corporation. This included evaluating and terminating, if necessary, management.

In 1992 I was approached by Robert Pugliese, general counsel to Westinghouse Electric Corporation, a manufacturing company in Pennsylvania. He told me that Westinghouse had self-destructed under a passive board, awakening only every three years or so to change CEOs. Under the circumstances, Pugliese sought help. The company's credit unit had overextended itself by doubling its loan assets to more than $13 billion. In 1993 I became more involved as things got really nasty—there had been huge write-offs on the bad loans, a credit downgrade, and internal revolts about big executive pay packages. There was even a sex scandal. CEO Paul Lego was allegedly "carrying on" with the head of Westinghouse corporate relations.

Bob told me stories which indicated that from the beginning Lego was on thin ice. I wasn't there at the time and have no personal knowledge of those events. As described in *Who Killed Westinghouse?*, in just two months before Lego took over as CEO in July 1990, he stunned the investment community by professing ignorance about details of the credit unit at a "routine" analyst meeting in Palm Beach. His predecessor, John Marous Jr., was still chairman and had been scheduled to go to the meeting but was out of town on an overseas trip. Lego confessed that the troubled unit, which reported to Marous, was the area of Westinghouse he knew "the least about." This was not reassuring from a man about to take the helm. After the stock fell $2, Marous called him the next day from Amsterdam.

"What the hell did you do?" he asked.

Lego replied he didn't do anything, that he just wasn't yet up to speed on what was going on at the financial services and credit units, because they reported directly to Marous. True, but not something to readily admit to analysts. Before long, Westinghouse took the first of three write-downs with a $975 million charge. The total would grow to $5.5 billion.

I had at the time been meeting on general governance matters with Richard Koppes, the general counsel of Cal-PERS. Westinghouse was one of its holdings, and Koppes told me, sidebar, that he was concerned management wasn't doing its job—a polite understatement.

There was a litany of questionable actions. Shortly after Lazard Frères warned that the troubles at the finance arm could lead to the firm's bankruptcy, an emergency meeting was called. But Lego was vacationing in Naples, Florida, and didn't want to go back to Pittsburgh, so two company G-IVs flew everyone down and back. Later, Lego hired Bob Watson from GE Capital to liquidate the financial services assets. Watson collected over $14 million for eighteen months of work.

Pugliese invited me to attend the July 1992 board meeting, and asked me to be painfully frank. I called out the handling of the credit problems, told the directors that major institutional investors were beating the drums, and pointed out that one of the board's primary obligations was to determine whether Westinghouse had the right CEO. What's more, I reported that if the directors didn't exercise their fiduciary duties and think hard about all of the company's problems, they could be liable. Things were that bad, and Bob and I thought serious warnings were needed to rouse the board.

Nobody said a word. Lego fumed, and afterward accused Bob of conspiring with me to embarrass him. The final straw came in late 1992, when Lego, despite heavy board pressure, turned down a partial bailout in which GE would acquire some of the loan portfolio, reducing Westinghouse's exposure, even though this was to be mostly a cherry-picking exercise with GE keeping most of the best loans. The board finally felt *something* had to be done—and so did the shareholder rights groups and pension funds that demanded Lego go.

It didn't take long. In early January, outside directors led by former Secretary of Defense Frank Carlucci and former Amoco Corp. chairman Richard Morrow began a series of conference calls to develop a quick exit strategy for Lego. After the customary dinner for directors and top managers at Pittsburgh's Duquesne Club the night before the January board meeting, which I was asked to attend, a director handed Executive Vice President Gary Clark an envelope. The note instructed Clark to meet with Morrow for early breakfast at the Hilton Hotel. At that breakfast, Morrow asked Clark to serve as interim CEO while the board looked for a permanent replacement for Lego. The board meeting lasted less than an hour. Lego was finally gone.

Again, a board publicly removed a CEO due to poor performance, rather than disguising it as a retirement, and showed corporate America that the board is in control. After GM, directors meeting alone and acting where necessary wasn't treason any more. The welfare of the corporation and its shareholders came before the potential for embarrassment.

Regardless of whether outside legal counsel is retained by the board to represent outside directors, or by management to represent the company, it is always helpful for outside counsel and the company's inside legal counsel to have a good working relationship built on mutual respect and trust for one another. The extent to which outside and inside legal counsel will work together will depend on the specific circumstances. I have been lucky. Like Harry Pearce at GM, Bob Pugliesi at Westinghouse was my partner in advising the board to act in the best interests of the company. As the years passed, more and more inside counsel have assumed the role of conscience of the corporation, not solely responsible to the CEO. It's a hard choice, but one that has now become the "norm" for general counsel.

Back at GM, the directors were well aware that replacing certain members of management was not enough to make all of GM's problems disappear. During the previous decade, GM's shareholders had lost faith in the company. Also, the directors struggled with how they could ensure that GM would not make the same mistakes it had in the past, including a board unable to make independent decisions and management that could not cope with its current circumstances. So the board and I met and we devised solutions to improve the company's corporate governance practices. These included addressing board-meeting efficiency, succession planning, professional development, independent directors meeting in the absence of management, annual director self-evaluations, and shareholder communications. While it may be common for today's boards to engage in these types of discussions, back when I was advising the GM board, it was almost unheard of.

Specifically, the directors, Harry Pearce, and I discussed establishing corporate governance guidelines for the effective governance of GM. Back then such guidelines pretty much didn't exist. In January 1994, the board issued the "Board Guidelines on Significant Corporate Governance Issues," designed to ensure active monitoring of management by an independent board.

The GM board adopted twenty-eight corporate governance guidelines that I helped develop with the guidance of the directors. They were critical to the establishment of a new environment of "best practices" at the auto giant. Key provisions included independent board leadership through a separate chairman or lead director, independent director executive sessions, and annual formal board evaluations. The guidelines codified many of the initiatives I had pressed for, including requiring that a substantial majority of directors be independent, that they have unrestricted access to management, and that they meet regularly on their own without management present. Requirements for an annual evaluation of the chairman and CEO, and a self-evaluation of the board itself and each of its committees, also ensured—at least in theory—the elimination of imperial CEO dominance and a new era of transparency between board members and top management. The GM corporate governance guidelines were called a Magna Carta for directors by the media and quickly gained the attention of corporate America.

The GM Corporate Governance Guidelines gained real traction when CalPERS embraced them. Rich Koppes, another fearless "inside" counsel, was there to plan with me how best to implement the work already done by the GM board to create effective corporate governance policies at other American corporations. In May 1994 CalPERS sent letters to the chairs of the largest two hundred domestic equity holdings within its portfolio. The letters challenged these companies to follow GM in conducting self-analysis and defining what would be important (or not) in their effort to improve corporate governance. CalPERS acknowledged that specific governance models may differ among corporations but encouraged boards to evaluate their processes and reflect upon their own corporate governance structure. In August, CalPERS sent a second letter to the companies that had failed to respond to its original request.

To give the survey some teeth, CalPERS embedded a clever follow-up mechanism: there would be no place to hide. The responses—spelling out what the companies were doing—would be analyzed, graded, and *published*. And CalPERS did what it said it was going to do. In September 1994 it published a report card for two hundred companies, with grades from A+ to F, based on the process by which the boards defined their structures and corporate governance practices. Of the two hundred companies, fourteen companies (7 percent) received an A+, while forty-one (20.5 percent) received an F for failing to respond to the letter. Those that received an A+ had submitted a comprehensive list of guidelines, with the board of directors being "clearly involved in the process."

The CalPERS survey received much attention, both from boards of directors and from the media. Companies with failing grades were criticized and forced to defend themselves. With the CalPERS initiative full steam ahead, in December 1994 CalPERS sent a third letter to the next hundred largest companies in its portfolio, asking them to respond to the corporate governance survey. Then in May 1995 CalPERS published its "Final Report," grading the three hundred companies' responses to the corporate governance challenge. Of these three hundred companies, eighty-six (29 percent) received an A+, while seventy-six (25 percent) received an F. What is noteworthy, and what signals to me that my efforts with CalPERS to engage large American corporations was successful, was that certain companies, like Allied Signal, Ameritech, Fleet Financial Group, and Gap originally received Fs for failing to respond to the survey but, in the 1995 Final Report, received an A+. The CalPERS corporate governance challenge encouraged directors to take their responsibilities seriously, which included evaluating their own board structure in an effort to implement effective corporate governance practices.

As meaningful change in governance standards gained momentum in the United States, new opportunity spread overseas. The Asian financial crisis that began with the collapse of the Thai baht in July 1997 undercut confidence in the markets and sent tremors around the world, hinting at a global economic meltdown. There was a jump in Asian private debt, more currency slumps, and sharp drops in stock market values. The International Monetary Fund put together a $40 billion program to stabilize currencies in

South Korea, Thailand, and Indonesia—where President Suharto was forced out after thirty years after a devaluation of the rupiah sharply increased prices.

The financial crisis in Asia brought to light the inefficiencies of the old way. Properly functioning capital markets are the key to economic and social well-being, which requires effective corporate governance—including transparent disclosure, investor protections, and responsible oversight of managers. Corporate governance—ensuring that managers are accountable to boards, which in turn are accountable to shareholders—is what makes access to capital possible, particularly for those companies in developing economies. A country must create an environment where foreigners feel it's safe to put their money. Lacking that, opportunities for investment, economic growth, and sustained value creation are limited. Properly governed companies can raise money at relatively low rates. Poorly governed companies pay casino rates.

In 1997 I received a call from Mats Isaksson, now head of corporate affairs at the Paris-based Organization for Economic Cooperation and Development (OECD), established in 1948 to help administer the Marshall Plan for rebuilding Europe. The organization now serves as a forum for thirty-four countries that exchange ideas and develop policies to enhance economic development.

Mats saw an opportunity for OECD to promote corporate governance on a global scale, particularly in emerging markets. He asked me to chair a new Business Sector Advisory Group on Corporate Governance (BSAG), set up by the OECD in 1996, to review and analyze international

Reprinted from:

BusinessWeek

April 13, 1998

HEADLINER: IRA MILLSTEIN

CORPORATE AMBASSADOR TO THE WORLD

Ira Millstein is packing up his corporate governance principles and taking them on the road. The governance maven and senior partner at Weil, Gotshal & Manges is leading a group that on Apr. 2 gave the Organization for Economic Cooperation & Development a set of recommendations that could dramatically change how non-U.S. companies are governed.

The report calls for smaller, more independent boards and argues that a company's central mission should be creating shareholder wealth. These aren't radical notions in the U.S., but they're a sharp departure from practices overseas. In Japan, boards are almost exclusively made up of insiders; in France, companies believe their commitments to employees and society are every bit as important as their responsibility to shareholders.

Assuming the OECD ministers approve the report, they'll urge companies to get on the bandwagon. But will the reforms take? Many management experts outside the U.S. are skeptical. That leaves investors to demand the same things they do in the U.S.

By John Byrne

Figure 4.2   Ira Millstein, chairman of OECD's Business Sector Advisory Group (1998).

corporate governance issues and to propose an agenda for OECD's future efforts (figure 4.2). My colleagues were Michel Albert, a member of the monetary policy council at the Banque de France; Sir Adrian Cadbury, the former chairman of Cadbury Schweppes; Robert Denham, the former chairman and CEO of Salomon Inc.; Dieter Feddersen, a German attorney and professor; and Nobuo Tateisi, chairman of Omron Corporation and a prominent Japanese businessman. We were dubbed the "six wise men" by the OECD and the media.

We quickly concluded that even beyond research, scores of meetings, phone calls, and colloquia with business leaders and institutional investors from OECD member countries to gain perspective and support, it was vital to generate some kind of driving principles. These weren't to be mandates, even if perceived to be by skeptical, if not resentful, governments. Pluralism and adaptability were critical, and it was important to come up with a road map of basic principles as the world adopted markets rather than government mandates, and capital was going global by nations trying to integrate into the world economy.

The wholesale adoption by any other country of U.S. and U.K. laws, regulations, and guidelines was neither possible nor desirable. The history and culture in which our legal, market, and governance systems evolved could not possibly be replicated elsewhere. Our layers of law, regulation, culture, and practice are *ours*—for better or worse. While we must examine the history of corporate governance in the United States and United Kingdom, this exercise was not to mimic, but to guide us, to learn from our achievements and our mistakes.

Far more important, in my view, was the study of the corporate governance codes that other industrialized countries—like Japan, Germany, and India—had developed, how those "best practices" worked, and how they compared in effectiveness. While the means varied, we found the goals remarkably similar. We hoped that our conclusions would be a benchmark of sorts for those countries that lacked the key underpinnings of effective capital markets: an efficient judicial system, stable government, and access to *reliable* economic and financial data.

In 1992 after a rash of high-profile business scandals, a British group called The Committee on the Financial Aspects of Corporate Governance published a report. In recent years London had suffered incidents of stock manipulation; outright theft of savers' funds by the CEOs of two investment firms; the siphoning of a conglomerate's funds into offshore companies owned by the CEO, who subsequently fled to Cyprus while out on bail; theft of employee pension funds by media baron Robert Maxwell; and the spectacular collapse of the Bank of Credit and Commerce International, liquidated after authorities concluded that the private bank had been soliciting deposits from drug dealers, money launderers, and terrorists.

The latter group included the infamous Abu Nidal, the leader of a renegade Palestinian terrorist group responsible for a string of assassinations, bombings, and hijackings. Nidal had an account with the BCCI branch in London. Unaware of Nidal's true identity, the branch manager took him to the shops to look for neckties—something that later prompted the memorable tabloid headline, "I Took Abu Nidal Shopping."

Chairing the "Cadbury Committee," as it quickly came to be known, was my friend Sir Adrian Cadbury, the former British Olympic rower and widely admired chairman of Cadbury Schweppes. His report, which was initially met with pushback from some in the British corporate world, was eventually widely embraced as a blueprint for corporate responsibility.

The *voluntary* code included several notable principles to improve board governance; for instance, that the chief executive and chairman positions should be split, the majority of the board should be comprised of outside directors, and the board should appoint three outside directors to form an audit committee. To the extent that the guidelines could be enforced, the code came under the London Stock Exchange requirement that listed companies had to "comply or explain." That meant that the companies had to either comply with the code, or if not, explain reasons for noncompliance.

In our own BSAG meetings, an important lightbulb went on. Based on our discussions with the OECD member countries and the international business community at large, we came to the realization that as nations throughout the world came to rely less on political control and more on market-driven economies, the competitive markets for capital were becoming truly global. As global competition for capital increases, capital will likely flow to those national economies and corporations that have adopted good governance standards, which include acceptable regulatory infrastructures, accounting and disclosure standards, satisfactory investor protections, and board practices designed to provide independent, accountable oversight of managers. So to catch the attention of the "world," we flatly linked corporate governance to access to capital. While developing countries might resist corporate governance, they couldn't ignore the need for capital. A link was established that none could control—everyone needs capital.

Our final report, delivered to the OECD's secretary general in April 1998, was titled "Corporate Governance: Improving Competitiveness and Access to Capital in Global Markets." The 107-page report reiterated our belief that there is no single universal model of corporate governance or final, static structure that every country or corporation should copy. Instead, there were four fundamental parameters to follow: fairness, transparency, accountability, and responsibility. Our recommendations included urging the OECD to issue a voluntary corporate governance "best practices code" designed to provide "minimum standards" of corporate governance to promote these four tenets (figure 4.3).

We also brushed the third-rail issue of "stakeholders," urging that the OECD emphasize the importance of social concerns and the need to clarify responsibilities between the public and private sectors. But we refrained from offering any specific advice or guidelines. Why? A common problem of having multiple stakeholders is that their interests often conflict, and can distract management from its principal mission—enhancing shareholder value over the long term. Because of our report, however, the OECD issued in May 1999 the *OECD Principles of Corporate Governance*, a set of nonbinding corporate governance standards and guidelines. These principles even today are recognized throughout the world as an international benchmark for policy makers and

Le Secrétaire général   2, rue André-Pascal
The Secretary General   75775 PARIS CEDEX 16
                                                          Tél. (33) 01 45 24 82 00
Ref: DJJ/98.295.bk   21 July 1998

Dear Ira,

Deputy Secretary-General Joanna Shelton is sending letters to members of the Business Sector Advisory Group, thanking them for their efforts in producing the report, "Corporate Governance: Improving Competitiveness and Access to Capital in Global markets." A copy of one of those letters is attached for your information. However, I want to take this opportunity to convey a special note of thanks to you as Chairman of the BSAG for the tremendous leadership you have shown in that project, as well as the important contribution you are making in our continuing efforts to develop OECD guidelines on corporate governance.

Your involvement in the OECD's work on corporate governance has helped us move from a stage where the issue was not even seen by many governments as an issue for public policymakers, to a point where our Ministers have asked us to prepare guidelines for the use of governments in shaping the corporate governance environment in Member countries -- guidelines which will be equally or more valuable for non-OECD countries. The work of the Business Sector Advisory Group, and the prior years of practice and expertise that you brought to its efforts, clearly will have a continuing impact on our work in this important area. This letter is hardly sufficient to thank you for the important contributions you already have made and the contributions yet to come, including as a key member of the ad hoc task force advising the Secretariat on the development of guidelines for corporate governance. However, I hope you will accept it as a sincere expression of our appreciation for the time, effort and commitment you have invested in this work.

Sincerely,

Donald J. Johnston

Encl.

Mr. Ira M. Millstein, P.C.
Senior Partner
Weil, Gotshal & Manges LLP
767 Fifth Avenue
New York, NY 10153-0119
U.S.A.

Figure 4.3 Thank you letter from Donald Johnston, secretary general of OECD, to Business Sector Advisory Group members (1998).

corporations, and they influence legislative and regulatory initiatives in both OECD and non-OECD countries.

There was a lot of initial head-nodding and some steps taken by foreign boards to embrace the principles, though some Asian OECD members were skeptical, preferring to handle things themselves. That approach wasn't particularly useful.

The May 1998 meeting of the G7 finance ministers focused on "strengthening the architecture" of the global finance system. The ministers specifically called on the World Bank—as a funder of long-term development—and the OECD to cooperate on developing a strategy to raise governance standards.

The OECD asked me to work with the World Bank to carry out the G7's directive, since I had previously advised the World Bank on various governance matters and understood the organization. So wearing my OECD hat, I approached James Wolfensohn, president of the World Bank. I had known Jim from his days at James D. Wolfensohn Inc., his investment firm that counseled an impressive list of major international and U.S. corporations. Jim had helped me out when I was advising the Macy's board on its debt problems. Our paths crossed earlier when Jim was executive partner and head of investment banking at Salomon Brothers.

Meeting in my conference room at Weil one day, Jim noticed my large painting of a cello by the post-cubist and constructivist artist Stephen Edlich. Jim took cello lessons from his friend, Jacqueline du Pré, in the mid-1970s, and was accomplished enough to perform at Carnegie Hall. He had to have the painting. I offered it to him as a gift.

Jim and I went about the task of linking the World Bank's international efforts to the governance principles of the OECD, this time focusing on developing countries. The aim was to blend the missions of both organizations: creating stable capital flows and fostering international cooperation, thereby reducing poverty and creating economic and social progress.

There were two formidable bureaucracies in our way. Getting a consensus from twenty-nine different nations on *anything* is difficult, but on as sensitive a subject as suggesting even general guidelines as to how to run their corporations, agreement on wording seemed impossible. Yet by June 1999, both groups had signed a memorandum of understanding that included the formation of a Private Sector Advisory Group (PSAG), a body that I would head.

Mats and I started to recruit: Ratan Tata, who ran India's most influential conglomerate; Jonathan Charkham, a former advisor to the Bank of England; Yoh Kurasawa, chairman of the Industrial Bank of Japan; and John Biggs, chairman and chief executive of TIAA-CREF, the huge U.S. investment firm that handled retirement accounts and services for educators and medical professionals, among others. We asked Adrian Cadbury to join us, but he declined—it was finally time for him to really retire. Our goal was to fill a vital gap in the global financial architecture by trying to make sense out of the fragmented, poorly coordinated, and often not well-understood or well-executed efforts at corporate reform around the world. Specifically, PSAG would advise on the educational efforts and development of regional and country-specific corporate governance programs to improve corporate governance practices in the private sector.

It was propitious timing. The world was still breathing the toxic fumes of the Asian financial crisis when traders sucked $100 billion of foreign capital out of Far East markets. Russia had depleted its currency reserves and defaulted on its debt. There were various pleas, seemingly everywhere, for bailouts, and widespread fears of "global contagion." It was increasingly clear that raising corporate governance standards internationally was critical to economic stability and sustainable growth. As Jim Wolfensohn told *The Economist*, "The governance of the corporation has become as important as the government of countries."

So we set about to implement a broad program of education and consultation, while making every effort to spur cooperation between the public and private sectors. As with the OECD principles, no one-size-fits-all solutions would be proposed. We aimed to drill down to the local policy makers and convince them how important foreign investment was to their long-term economic strength.

Part of our strategy was to recruit business leaders from developed countries to go out and make the case, realizing how much more persuasive and credible they would be than a bunch of bureaucrats or academics. We convinced several luminaries to do this, including John Bogle, chairman of The Vanguard Group; Dr. William Crist, chairman of CalPERS; Robert Pelosky Jr., managing director at Morgan

Stanley; and Alastair Ross Goobey, CEO of Hermes Pensions Management. The overall plan included a series of "Policy Dialogue Roundtables" in Russia, Asia, Latin America, and Africa. The idea was to broaden the debate and make everyone aware of governance issues by providing a regular forum for representatives of the region's public and private sectors. We would encourage candid discussion of governance experiences and hope to expand the network of governance advocates and contribute to the reform efforts in specific countries. We set up an investor task force of individuals from some of the most recognized names in the investment community—representing more than $3 trillion in capital—to instruct emerging economies on the need for long-term capital flow and governance reform. The PSAG continues today.

For years I spread the OECD gospel—in May 1999 Fritz Heimann, the former associate general counsel of General Electric Company, invited me to attend a meeting in Washington to consider how to assist a group called Transparency International to determine its next steps in combating fraud and bribery. Transparency International is a Berlin-based nonprofit that monitors and publicizes corporate and political corruption through a network of locally established chapters that uncover corruption—everything from small bribes to large-scale looting—any action that abuses entrusted power for private gain.

The SEC, Treasury, the then–Big Five accounting firms, DuPont, GE, Bethlehem Steel, the World Bank, the International Monetary Fund, and the Federal Reserve all attended.

This was the perfect forum to push the cooperative governance efforts of the OECD and World Bank.

Everyone agreed: transparency and disclosure were the keys to eliminating fraud and bribery, along with accurate financial information and good corporate ethics. With that, there could be better access to global capital and financial services. Nobody expected overnight miracles but they were hopeful. I apprised them of the governance initiatives that were underway internationally, including the cooperative efforts of the OECD and the World Bank. This was well received and everyone thought the OECD Principles of Corporate Governance could be the foundation of worldwide reform.

It took a while, but in a landmark decision in November 2015, all the leaders of the G20 countries endorsed corporate governance standards that Mats Isaksson and I had sketched during endless walks and talks in Paris and New York, now updated as "G20/OECD Principles of Corporate Governance."

"This truly global and high-level political backing shows that what we, together with Sir Adrian Cadbury, put in motion so many years ago had stood the test of time," says Mats. "It has only grown in importance as finance and business has become more and more international."

After spending more than a decade creating change in the boardroom, working with both the business community and institutional investors, and counseling boards of directors, I realized that many directors wanted to follow in the footsteps of GM and play a more active role in the governance of their corporations. They simply didn't have the experience to know how; their attitudes were rooted in the past.

So I turned to teaching and writing to provide directors and their advisors with what I had learned. In addition, I sought to engage academia in considering the foundations of corporate governance. At the heart of my thinking was this: boards are the fulcrum of accountability in the system and my experiences might be instructive to help them carry out their responsibilities.

Why is the board the focal point? When I started teaching what I think was the first course called "Corporate Governance" at Harvard Kennedy School in the early 1980s, it covered a potpourri of issues, like securities and antitrust law, shareholder derivative litigation, and takeover battles. It took a few terms of organizing and teaching the course before I realized how elegantly our corporate laws had created a chameleon—the modern corporation—capable of changing to fit the times. The board of directors was at the core of this legal creation, empowered to oversee the corporation's affairs, hire and fire the managers, set the corporation's strategic course, and most important, change the corporation's organization and management in a variety of ways. Teaching continued at Yale and Columbia, and I adopted President Clinton's approach before he did, and posted in my head the slogan to remember—"It's the Board, Stupid."

With that slogan and other writings in mind, I published in the American Bar Association's business law journal, the *Business Lawyer*, "The Evolution of the Certifying Board" (1993), "The Professional Board" (1995), and "The Responsible Board" (1997). I recommended putting directors in a position to "certify" to shareholders that the CEO is evaluated regularly and is doing what the board expects; that the board has people with the combined professional skill sets to address substantive areas like strategic planning and executive compensation; and that the board assumes the critical role of balancing social demands and expectations alongside profit maximization for shareholders, in other words, integrating "extrinsics" into the decision-making process. (To continue to educate and empower directors, I wrote several books and articles regarding the role and responsibilities of directors. These include *The Recurrent Crisis in Corporate Governance* (with Paul W. MacAvoy, Palgrave MacMillan, 2003) and "The Active Board of Directors and Performance of the Large Publicly Traded Corporation" (with Paul W. MacAvoy, *Columbia Law Review* 98:1283–1322), which show the correlation between an independent board and strong company performance.)

The *Business Lawyer* articles gained quick traction. For example, the "Report of the NACD Blue Ribbon Commission on Director Professionalism" that was published in 1996, noted that "[w]hen we saw Ira Millstein's article on 'The Professional Board' . . . we knew the time was right to form a Blue Ribbon Commission on this subject."

Passionate boards must be continually educated to improve their own performance. So when the NACD asked me to chair its Blue Ribbon Commission on Director Professionalism, I agreed. Similar to the earlier Business Roundtable statements, I made clear that the commission's report was not meant to impose "fixed, rigid rules." Rather, it was a guide for directors to consider instilling professionalism, the thought that being a director was not a job for amateurs.

(My work extended from educating boards of directors on their roles and responsibilities to educating board committees, including cochairing the Blue Ribbon Committee on Improving the Effectiveness of Corporate Audit Committees and publishing in 1999 the "Report and Recommendations of the Blue Ribbon Committee on Improving the Effectiveness of Corporate Audit Committees.")

The blueprints are here. They just need to be followed and adopted, board by board. Too much education on these matters is never enough. One corporation that never even went to class, let alone looked at the blueprints, was Drexel Burnham Lambert, home to the junk bond king Michael Milken.

5

DREXEL: THE MOST FEARED FIRM ON WALL STREET

O ther than the implosion of Lehman Brothers, no Wall Street meltdown has received more attention over the years than the collapse of Drexel Burnham Lambert. Once a modest Philadelphia brokerage firm, it grew to $2.3 billion in capital and had become what *Forbes* called "the terror of Wall Street." When it all began to unravel, I was in the middle of it. My client was Drexel's CEO, Fred Joseph.

Drexel is a chilling example of what can happen when directors play a passive role in the governance of the corporation, looking the other way and failing to ask the tough questions. When those entrusted to protect the corporation were finally ready to provide much-needed oversight, it was too late and there was no turning back.

Mine was an excellent perch from which to watch a good thing going wrong. After the firm had collapsed, a small group of us successfully orchestrated an unprecedented global settlement involving hundreds of claims asserted against Drexel in federal court. Judge Milton Pollack, who handled the case, called me the "arch manipulator"—but more about that later. I knew the settlement was in the best interests of all parties, if for no other reason than that nobody liked it. You know you have a good settlement when everyone walks away annoyed.

Drexel earned its bad-boy reputation by rising to power as the dominant, often ruthless market maker in high-yield securities. Led by the brilliant Michael Milken, a driven man who knew how to move only at ramming speed, "junk bonds" had become the coin of the realm in the 1980s for high-profile hostile takeovers and leveraged buyouts (LBOs), including Drexel's tumultuous but ultimately successful $25 billion deal on behalf of KKR for RJR Nabisco.

The Drexel story holds several instructive corporate governance lessons. The first is to lock the barn door *before* the horse escapes. Milken avoided any danger of real oversight by moving his entire junk bond trading operation to Beverly Hills in 1978. He was totally off the New York radar, out on his own, doing whatever he wanted to do. There was awe and envy back at 60 Broad Street over the unstoppable money machine Milken appeared to be running—and there was increasing scorn from older Drexel bankers who felt that Milken was just a peddler in a fancy suit selling damaged goods from his pushcart. But this was Wall Street: greed prevailed. There was so much honey flowing into the pot from Beverly Hills that nobody wanted to imperil the pipeline by asking too many questions. Instead, executives and directors who had the power to rein Milken in ignored their oversight responsibilities.

It was much the same a few years later at Kidder, Peabody & Co., where top executives were desperate to impress

Kidder's parent, General Electric. To do that, they had to prove to Jack Welch that they could return the firm to its former glory as a "silk collar" investment bank, one of whose early clients was AT&T. Under such profit pressure, nobody stopped to ask why the fixed-income unit suddenly seemed to be printing money, contributing $210 million—almost half—of the firm's $439 million profits in 1993.

As it turned out, those profits were counterfeit. They were based on the fraud of a single trader, Joseph Jett, who initiated but never closed billions of dollars of trades, creating a Ponzi-like cascade of rollovers. As a scathing report by attorney Gary Lynch, the former chief of the SEC's Enforcement Division, noted: "Time and again questions (about Jett's unusual trading profits) were answered incorrectly, ignored, or evaded." One important reason for those oversights, the report said, was Jett's importance to Kidder's bottom line: "As his profitability increased, skepticism about Jett's activities was often dismissed or unspoken."

Drexel's flow of junk bonds also provided the easiest way for companies with less than great credit to tap the lending market, particularly those with promising new technologies. That was not all bad for innovation—when it worked. MCI, Turner Broadcasting, and McCaw Cellular all jumped in. Milken and his high-profile supporters—mainly the editorialists at *The Wall Street Journal*—claimed that the junk-bond phenomenon generated thousands of new jobs and gave an important push to the economy. But one could also argue that the junk-fueled LBO craze had another side—the new leveraged owners often had to lay off workers and forgo investments in order to meet the steep coupon payments.

Undisputed, however, was the fact that junk bonds made numerous people fabulously wealthy, including, of course, Milken, whose family's net worth reportedly reached $3 billion in 1986.

The concept of high-yield bonds was hardly new, going back to the early days of the republic, when raising money for the Treasury was a key priority. To jumpstart their early financings, high-yield issuers in the first decades of the twentieth century included General Motors, IBM, and U.S. Steel. But after the industrial economy was firmly established, "investment grade" bonds—lower yields but less risk—dominated the markets until the 1970s. It was then that the Arab oil embargo, inflation, and higher interest rates doubled the cost of short-term borrowing. Investors scurried out of equities into money market funds, which now paid attractive double-digit returns. A bear-market mentality prevailed, and in 1974, the Dow Jones Industrial Average fell 45 percent to the bottom of a 20-year range. The resulting credit crunch cut off an important source of funds for all but those whose debt securities were at the very top of the Moody's and S&P's "AAA" ratings lists.

Milken saw opportunity in adversity: High-yield bonds, he figured, would attract both borrowers (better liquidity, he claimed), and investors (yields averaged 14.5 percent, typically 300 to 400 basis points more than for U.S. Treasuries). It has been said that Milken cherry-picked one highly qualified conclusion from an old book about bond quality, and used it as the basis for his gospel: that below-investment–grade debt earned a higher risk-adjusted rate of return than investment-grade bonds.

This was only partly correct. As author Ben Stein noted in his 1992 book, *A License to Steal*, what Milken neglected to mention was that the same bond quality book also pointed out that the time period studied (1900 to 1943) was highly unusual. Bonds bought for phenomenally low prices during the Depression showed fantastic gains during the rearmament boom of World War II, "when there were essentially no defaults, there were many, many calls at above par, and some securities that had been exchanged for defaulted bonds rose spectacularly in value." But why let facts get in the way of a good sales pitch?

The publicly traded high-yield market grew to nearly $180 billion by the end of the 1980s, up from $10 billion a decade before. Privately placed high-yield securities added another $150 billion to this astonishing total. Drexel commanded a dominant percentage of both markets and was also the biggest player in the high-yield secondary market, trading in more than fifteen hundred such issues, worth over $125 billion.

Drexel and Milken got rich. In 1986, Drexel became Wall Street's most profitable firm, earning $545 million on revenues of more than $4 billion. At one point, Milken himself was earning close to $600 million a year. The bonus pool for the high-yield department in 1986 was $700 million. As the chief dispenser, Milken passed out $150 million to his colleagues, then kept $550 million for himself, more than the whole firm itself had earned that year.

Drexel was a private firm owned largely by its employees, so there was little incentive for all the staffers to ask tough questions as they were getting rich. On its face this presented a huge bar to responsible oversight, a common mindset on the profit-obsessed street. This mindset is worth repeating: if the money pit is filling up, don't jeopardize the source. It was far from the ideal setting for corporate governance, which requires a coordinated process for active and independent oversight.

My involvement with Drexel began in November 1986 when Fred Joseph asked me to be his personal lawyer. I was recommended to Fred by Gershon Kekst, a close friend of both of ours who was concerned about Fred (figure 5.1). Gershon told me that he had a high regard for Fred and wanted a lawyer who would be sensitive as well as tough minded. There were all sorts of rumors swirling about Milken and the firm, especially since two people with close ties to Drexel had pleaded guilty to securities fraud. Anyone at his level would be concerned.

Dennis Levine, a Drexel banker, was one of the first caught up in a major insider trading scandal prosecuted by Rudy Giuliani, then the U.S. attorney for the Southern District of New York. Another of Giuliani's targets was Ivan Boesky, the arbitrageur who often did business with Milken. After his guilty plea, Boesky cooperated with the SEC and the Justice Department during their ongoing parallel investigations. It didn't take long for Milken's name to come out. Soon the trail led right to his Beverly Hills office.

Sitting in Fred's 60 Broad Street office, just down the street from the New York Stock Exchange, Fred asked me to listen in on his phone conversations with Milken. Milken talked expansively about his trading, how he wooed new clients and how he would "restructure" the debt by relying

Figure 5.1   Ira Millstein poses with Gershon Kekst (2002).

on what journalist James B. Stewart described as a "new and dazzling array of high-yield securities to replace the debt that was on the verge of default. The new tiers invariably pushed payments further into the future, giving the company more time to revive, and forestalling any rise in default rates."

For companies like the California savings and loans associations (S&Ls) and insurance companies that Milken loaded with debt, this was a predestined disaster, particularly after a 1988 published study by researchers at the Harvard Graduate School of Management proved that the default rate on junk was roughly three times what Milken claimed. To Milken and his apologists, it was a devastating rejection of all the prior academic "proof" that junk bonds enjoyed a low rate of default. For fiduciaries like insurers and pension funds entrusted with other peoples' money, this meant that they *theoretically* would have to set aside new reserves for possible defaults, report lower earnings, and pay out lower interest on whatever products they offered.

But Milken was treating the junk bond market as his personal billion-dollar casino. He controlled it totally, knew where every bond was, and where to buy and sell when he needed to. As was alleged in various documents surrounding the later guilty pleas, Milken would often "overfund" offerings by as much as 100 percent, convincing his clients to invest the excess in other companies' junk bonds, which of course Milken eagerly provided. He would sell the same security at the same time to different people at different prices. He would trade tens of billions at will, fixing both ends of the trade to give himself whatever profits or commissions he wanted. Congressional investigators determined that

Milken routinely sold new junk issues to himself, then resold them to his "captive" S&Ls and insurers at a substantial premium.

Though I was convinced that Fred had no criminal exposure, I was not at all sure about Milken. What he was doing didn't sit right with me. So I personally, more than once, urged Fred that it would be in his best interest to resign and take whatever money he was entitled to. To Fred, this was unacceptable. He brushed aside my concerns and did little more than fret privately.

Over the next two years, the firm and Milken faced charges of insider trading, stock manipulation, and tax law violations. A federal grand jury indicted Milken on criminal racketeering charges and sought $1.8 billion in forfeitures from him and other defendants.

Previously, RICO charges were rarely pressed except for mob cases, but here Giuliani used it as a powerful weapon to go after those he said were Wall Street's major villains. Fred feared that a RICO charge against the firm itself, certainly a possibility, would be a death sentence for Drexel.

The firm pleaded with the Justice Department not to head down that road, or to bring any criminal charges at all. The firm outlined a death-spiral scenario to the top prosecutors: Drexel's short-term lenders, who supplied funds for daily operating expenses, would pull the financing that accounted for 90 percent of the firm's $29 billion assets. Underwriting income would disappear. After all, who wants to deal with a firm that's been labeled a racketeer? Key "rainmakers" would defect. There would be a run on the firm's $1.1 billion of equity capital owned by employee shareholders.

Whether these arguments had any influence or not is unclear, but in the end, the Justice Department brought no RICO charges against Drexel. Right as the grand jury reportedly was voting on an indictment, Drexel entered an "Alford plea," in which a criminal defendant files a guilty plea but asserts his innocence while admitting that the evidence would likely persuade a judge or jury to convict. Drexel agreed to pay a record $650 million fine. The next month, the firm settled with the SEC, agreeing to stricter safeguards on oversight procedures. Five thousand jobs, including those of all the retail brokers, were eliminated.

Realizing the firm was in deep trouble, I suggested to Fred that we set up a new board committee known as the Oversight Committee. He quickly agreed. We recruited two former heads of the SEC, John Shad and Roderick Hills, as well as Ralph Saul, the former head of the American Stock Exchange, who previously headed up the trading and markets division of the SEC. We hoped this lineup would convince the Justice Department, the SEC, the New York Federal Reserve Bank, and the Treasury that Drexel was serious about reforming and had every intention to stay in business.

Yet the damage had already been done. The squeaky clean new leadership made little difference to the New York Federal Reserve Bank, the Treasury Department, or other Wall Street firms, which continued to demonize Drexel and scale back their business dealings with the firm that had become anathema. It was too little, too late. Regulators, investors, and the press saw this after-the-fact new governance environment as just another cynical Wall Street example of putting lipstick on the pig. This is another major corporate governance lesson out of the Drexel mess: sometimes it's just too late to fix things.

Turmoil in the junk bond market in the fall of 1989 and early 1990, plus two downgrades of its commercial paper rating, strapped Drexel of cash, in part because it had also been liquidating its own capital in order to buy back junk inventories from its clients—an odd strategy Ben Stein called "buying back the Brooklyn Bridge." The firm posted a $40 million loss for 1989—the first operating loss in its 54-year history.

There seemed to be only two options left—a cash infusion by the banks or a bailout by the Treasury. Neither happened. The banks met but didn't commit. Fred was convinced that regulators would call the banks and tell them to help us. But the regulators put no pressure on the banks to lend. Neither was there any hope of a Treasury bailout, not with Nicholas Brady as the Secretary. Brady, who was previously at Dillon Read, had been advising Fred Hartley's Unocal on its defense strategy against a failed hostile takeover bid by T. Boone Pickens's Mesa Petroleum—financed largely by Drexel junk bonds. Brady had little sympathy for Drexel. Regulators, including SEC Chairman Richard Breeden, ordered Drexel to file for bankruptcy the night of February 12, 1990, threatening to commence a Securities Investor Protection Corporation proceeding if Drexel did not agree. But one of my partners, Alan Miller, said, "I can't file tonight, we haven't got the papers." So we obtained a twenty-four-hour extension, filing for bankruptcy on February 13. Fred left Drexel soon after the company filed for bankruptcy. By that time, Milken had resigned and was forming his own financial consulting firm.

The RICO charges against Milken were ultimately dropped—he pleaded guilty to six felony charges of securities fraud and conspiracy, and agreed to pay an astounding $600 million in fines and penalties. "I transgressed certain of the laws and regulations that govern our industry," Milken told the court. "I was wrong in doing so and knew that at the time, and I am pleading guilty to these offenses."

In sentencing Milken, Federal Judge Kimba Wood showed little mercy. "Your crimes show a pattern of skirting the law, stepping just over to the wrong side of the law in an apparent effort to get some of the benefits from violating the law without running a substantial risk of being caught," she said. "This kind of misuse of your leadership position and enlisting employees who you supervised to assist you in violating the law are serious crimes warranting serious punishment and the discomfort and opprobrium of being removed from society."

The sentence: ten years. At first it didn't register, but outside the courtroom, Milken burst into tears when he finally realized what he was facing. The sentence was subsequently reduced and Milken wound up spending only twenty-two months in jail, but was banned for life from the securities industry.

For me, the hard work was just beginning. We started working on Drexel's bankruptcy settlement in 1990, and by the fall of 1991, there were over 150 pending federal civil lawsuits against Drexel, its managers, and Milken, plus the claims of more than nine thousand creditors in the bankruptcy proceeding. The prospect of an unimaginable number of claims involving so many complex issues that would take years to resolve, with uncertain results, and the prospect of serious statute of limitation problems, was simply unacceptable to plaintiffs and defendants alike. To adjudicate the claims expediently, Judge Milton Pollack gave his blessing to proceed with something nobody thought was practical: negotiating an agreement by all parties on a voluntary settlement. The defendants would deny any liability, but the plaintiffs could recover some $2 billion, mostly from the resolution of the bankruptcy proceedings.

All agreed it seemed impossible, but everyone had to make it work or face years of uncertainty. It would not have been possible without the proactive involvement of Judge Pollack, who made himself constantly available to the lawyers by phone. After obtaining everyone's consent, he also met privately with attorneys without other parties present. This remarkable gesture—handing out free *ex parte* passes—injected integrity and trust into the process. Everyone had to behave under the constant glare of Judge Pollack. It was something I had never experienced in my decades of practice before the federal bench.

Judge Pollack also saved the day, over and over, with last-minute cajoling. In February of 1992, when everyone thought the negotiations were resolved, some last-minute collateral issues came up. The judge somehow managed to get another $150 million in fresh cash posted as security. I'd never seen a jurist do that kind of active duty before. Later that same month, the lawyers held a press briefing to announce that everyone had reached agreement.

Then, just when everything seemed to be resolved, the settlement almost didn't happen, jeopardizing years of work. Melvyn Weiss, the lawyer who managed about half of the forty or so class-action suits around the country, brought up his attorney fees. Weiss wanted Pollack, once the settlement was done, to send each class action case back to its individual court to set the fees. Weiss could of course then approach the separate courts himself and argue before each judge for as much as he could get. To save time and money, I strongly argued that the fee decision should be Judge Pollack's alone. But Weiss, probably correctly assuming that he would get less money that way, said that option was a deal breaker.

Everyone was irate, including me. We had all worked so hard to get where we were. I was upset to the point that I left the room to cool down. David Boies, then of Cravath, Swaine & Moore, one of the lawyers representing the Federal Deposit Insurance Corporation, helped me calm down and come back to the table, asserting that I was needed to get the deal done. In the end, Weiss reportedly had a conversation with the judge that gave him leeway to go back to the individual courts. But the agreement did not guarantee that at all, so I guess we all let it go at that.

On March 2, 1992, his courtroom was packed with over a hundred dark suits and scores of fourteen-pound wingtips for the hearing that everyone had thought would never come. Judge Pollack addressed the stunning assembly of legal talent—including Arthur Liman, who had attempted to have Judge Pollack disqualified—and declared that the last of the bankruptcy issues were resolved and that the global settlement was just a step or two away from the finish line. Here was the last "or forever hold your peace" moment for anyone who wanted to lodge an eleventh-hour complaint.

A few lawyers spoke, but a lot of what some of them had to say related to bankruptcy and not the settlement, prompting a polite but firm cutoff from the judge. Others claimed that their clients had not participated in the settlement talks or didn't think they were getting enough money. That did not go over well with His Honor.

"There is no compulsion to require you to participate," he said. "It's voluntary, and if you don't like the terms, my advice is to tell your client you don't like the terms. See if you can get better terms somewhere, somehow in this century."

The deed was done. Drexel no longer existed. Milken was in jail, his Beverly Hills office vacant and for rent. Fred Joseph was never charged with any crimes. But because of his failure to ensure that Milken's high-yield department obeyed securities laws, Joseph was censured and banned for two years from serving as a supervisor or manager at any NYSE member firm. He eventually returned to Wall Street and cofounded a small investment bank that worked with midsized companies. He and Milken never spoke again.

The saga ended as well as it could have under the circumstances. It serves as a warning of the importance of governance systems in the financial markets. Has anyone learned the lesson? Looking at the more than $100 billion in fines and penalties paid by financial institutions following the crisis of 2008, one could say, "Not yet." Companies still need oversight in these complex structures.

But I am not suggesting that governance problems are limited to the private sector. No matter what the context, when nobody is supervising, trouble and mischief inevitably come calling.

6

DEAD BROKE: NEW YORK CITY'S 1970S FISCAL CRISIS

I n the fall of 1975, New York City no longer had enough money to pay its garbage collectors, firefighters, and cops. That is to say nothing of meeting the enormous interest payments due on the billions in outstanding loans and bonds the city had issued over the previous decade to float its operating budget.

Albany politicians, Wall Street banks, and bond lawyers had happily enabled the city. They used devices like "revenue anticipation bonds" or "tax anticipation notes," crossing their fingers that the anticipated bond or tax income would cover near-term operating expenses. They hoped that more such bonds could always be sold. There was an unwillingness of overseers (in this case, enablers) to face the facts, not unlike entrenched boards and managers ignoring change and watching competitors win the game. New York City's fiscal crisis is an example of what can happen, even to a city that is at the epicenter of the financial markets, when there are no controls or systems of checks and balances to monitor and curb excessive spending. Vigilance and oversight on behalf of those to whom you are responsible, is what corporate governance is all about. This time a city's welfare was at stake.

This out-of-control spending machine, embraced *in extremis* by John Lindsay, the mayor in the late 1960s who too often gave in to the demands of the city's powerful unions, was the fiscal time bomb that Abraham D. Beame— a pleasant man, someone who looked very much like the accountant he was trained to be—inherited. At only 5'2", he was small in stature, but large in ambition and in his devotion to New York.

Though he was passive and would sit through important city hall meetings without saying a word, Beame, very much a nuts-and-bolts man who focused on the mechanics of city government rather than on visionary urban planning, was the product of the city's Democratic machine, which rose to power through bribes, threats, patronage, and a highly efficient voter-turnout effort. To my knowledge, Beame was never attached to the seamy side of the New York Democratic Party. But the leaders of the city's five boroughs—Manhattan, Brooklyn, the Bronx, Queens, and Staten Island—were pulling the strings. Around this time, one of the city's most colorful political operatives was Carmine DeSapio. DeSapio wore tinted glasses, dressed impeccably in tailored dark suits and striped ties, and always spoke calmly, rarely raising his voice. My impression was that he at times operated in a gray area, but he vigorously denied any links to organized crime.

He was the perfect image of an intimidating and unapproachable man in power, and many people were afraid to talk to him. "Mr. DeSapio," people would say nervously. Never "Carmine." It was widely and publicly rumored that

DeSapio was selling judgeships and cozying up to local members of the mob. I didn't know the specifics, but I wasn't surprised at the rumors.

The U.S. Senate's famed Kefauver Committee, which investigated organized crime, concluded that the mobster Frank Costello heavily influenced the policies of DeSapio's Tammany Hall machine, which ruled Manhattan. DeSapio testified that while he had met Costello several times, "We never discussed politics."

DeSapio was convicted in 1969 of conspiring to bribe the former city water commissioner and of extorting contracts from Consolidated Edison in exchange for kickbacks. Former Mayor Edward Koch, a frequent DeSapio critic, nonetheless said many years later: "He's a crook, but I like him."

It was an era of political capitalism, where the machine, not the public, ran the city. The public effectively had no vote on who would be mayor. Instead they voted for whomever the bosses put up. There were rarely any "accidental" political appointments. The bosses had to approve everyone, and the litmus test was unquestioning loyalty. Anyone who gave even a hint of disloyalty was gone. It wasn't pretty—but it continued because the public was both apathetic about voting and enjoyed watching the machine at work.

Beame wanted badly to be mayor—and said so. He carried around crumpled pieces of paper with microscopic handwriting spelling out policies he would implement. He once even tucked them into his bathing suit. What would have happened to his political agenda had he gone in the water?

Beame, who was well liked, had spent several years in the city comptroller's office, making his ambitions known within the machine, which finally agreed to put him forward in 1973 against the Republican candidate, State Senator John Marchi. Beame won decisively with 56.49 percent of the citywide vote. His legacy from Lindsay included not only suffocating debt, but also the habit of borrowing, which snowballed.

Because of his alleged expertise in accounting, Beame ran with the slogan, "He Knows the Buck." But the reality was he didn't expect the looming crisis from the Lindsay years. In February 1975, a little more than a year into his administration, the city planned another round of money raising, this time attempting to raise $260 million in short-term notes borrowed against taxes that were due the next month.

Five years earlier, a young lawyer's questions at a closing had scuttled a $120 million loan from First Boston to the Penn Central, which caused the railroad to file for bankruptcy. This time, Marion J. Epley III, a thirty-eight-year-old junior partner from White & Case, representing Banker's Trust, which headed the syndicate for the bond offering, insisted that City Comptroller Harrison J. Goldin certify financial data for the current receipts—not just those for the previous month, which was established practice. Goldin couldn't produce it. Banker's Trust withdrew from the deal, as did the other main members of the underwriting: Citibank and Chase Manhattan. David Rockefeller, who ran Chase and was the de facto head of the New York banking community, said no, politely but firmly.

That was the tipping point. No other bank, New York State, or the federal government would step forward with bailout money. Beame summoned Charles Seligson, my law partner, whom I accompanied to city hall. We were asked to attend because Seligson and Beame shared ties to Brooklyn. Seligson asked me to come because it was city hall—not his usual jurisdiction. Seligson, properly referred to as "Professor," was uneasy in that atmosphere, which was new to him—not that I was that familiar with the situation or the other players. Beame trusted Seligson and therefore assumed he could trust me. From then on, I was an advisor, pro bono.

I often met with First Deputy Mayor John Zuccotti, the competent and hardworking deputy who effectively operated as de facto mayor in those frequent times when Beame was frozen in indecision. Zuccotti was trusted by the financial community and was a key to New York City's survival. I liked Beame, but his actions were foreign to me. In one meeting that dragged on well beyond the dinner hour in the basement of Gracie Mansion, the mayor's home on the Upper East Side overlooking the East River, his wife, Mary, came in and said, "Mayor Beame, I have your dinner ready." Not "Abe" but "Mayor Beame." Beame rose without a word and went to have his dinner, leaving me with Zuccotti and Howard Rubenstein (who advised the mayor on public relations) with some potato chips and Coca-Cola.

First I wanted access to the city's books. So I asked James Cavanagh, a deputy mayor who orchestrated the city's various financial maneuvers, where the books were. "There are no books," he said. All Cavanagh seemed to have were "notes."

Figure 6.1 Susan Zuccotti, John Zuccotti, Susan Frame Millstein, and Ira Mill-stein, almost forty years after the New York City fiscal crisis, at the American Red Cross of Greater New York Ball (2011).

I was incredulous. "There are *no books*? But what happens if you run out of money?"

Cavanagh's answer: "We just go to Albany." That meant another bond issue or some new piece of smoke-and-mirrors legislation that would temporarily postpone an interest pay-ment deadline. Neither of those options were viable now. I was no financial expert, so I went looking for one.

J. C. Penney was a client of Weil's, and with the help of my partners, we recruited Kenneth S. Axelson, director of finance at J. C. Penney, for the job. The city clearly could not afford to pay Axelson, so I approached J. C. Penney Chair-man William M. Batten, and asked if the city could "borrow" Axelson for a couple years. Batten, a great citizen, agreed and "loaned" Axelson to the city for one dollar a year. Axelson was named deputy mayor for finance, and with Weil partner Carl Lobell, drafted a financial plan for New York City.

October 16, 1975 was the night of the Alfred E. Smith Memorial Foundation Dinner, an annual white-tie charitable fundraiser at the Waldorf Astoria honoring Al Smith, the first Catholic presidential candidate. The dinner, sponsored by the Archdiocese of New York, provides a stage every four years for the presidential contenders and an outlet for humor—like George W. Bush's remark during his first campaign, "This is an impressive crowd. The haves and the have-mores. Some people call you the elite. I call you my base."

Given the perilous state of the city, several of us assembled back at Weil later that night to discuss the looming crisis. It was clear to Harvey Miller, our lead bankruptcy partner, that we must confront the mayor and the assemblage with a clear picture of the pending doom. So we set off for Gracie Mansion. Our message was blunt. "You're broke. You're not going to be able to meet payroll tomorrow, the banks are going to set off [seize the city's money], and if they do that, there won't be a penny anywhere because whatever you have on deposit will be gone." Zuccotti backed us.

The city needed $450 million the next day to meet its payroll and notes due, hoping for the sale of $400 million in Municipal Assistance Corporation bonds to the city's municipal employee pension funds. But the sale was derailed at the eleventh hour by Albert Shanker, the combative president of the United Federation of Teachers, the teacher's union. Shanker said the pension trustees wouldn't agree because they might be sued for a breach of fiduciary duty for investing in what they perceived were low-quality bonds.

Shanker, with his reputation for organizing teacher strikes as the first—rather than last—resort, was immortalized in the classic 1973 Woody Allen futuristic film *Sleeper*, in which one of the characters casually explains that the entire southeastern United States had been destroyed "over a hundred years ago" when "a man named Albert Shanker got hold of a nuclear warhead."

The mayor resisted reality. He said, again and again, "It can't happen, it can't happen. They'll never do it. They'll never throw us into bankruptcy. Impossible." The only way out, we explained, was to persuade the unions to buy bonds. Failing that, we must prepare for the worst. We returned to the office and Harvey Miller drafted, or rather, invented, a petition under state law to file a repayment plan for approximately $7.8 billion in serial bonds and sinking fund bonds and almost $5 billion in short-term debt, mostly made of the "anticipation" bonds. Nobody had ever filed a petition like this before. I've hung the signed petition in my office, and it will be donated to the New York Historical Society, as a reminder of what can happen when there are essentially no checks and no balances in place. The petition was to support an "order" staying the banks from "setting off" against the city funds that we held.

The process certainly wasn't a classic federal bankruptcy filing—which would have been unmanageable—but it would have had the same practical effect. It was an admission by the city that it was broke, for sure. Not only did we then have to convince the mayor to sign it, but we also had to ask a state judge to approve the petition and stay order—that same night.

At about 10:30 p.m., the mayor asked John Zuccotti to call Washington. Zuccotti told the White House operator that the mayor of New York City had an urgent matter to discuss with President Ford—but he was told that the president was already asleep. "I'll call you back," Zuccotti said. "What do you want me to do now?" Zuccotti asked the mayor. "Leave a message for him," Beame replied. So Zuccotti called back and said, "President Ford should know that New York City will probably file for bankruptcy in the morning."

Perhaps a hint of things to come—including the famous *New York Daily News* headline, "Ford to City: Drop Dead"— the president never called back.

Back to Gracie Mansion. Again Harvey and I had to tell the mayor that the city was broke. Beame kept wanting me, and everyone assembled, to tell him there was something that he could do other than sign the petition. Unfortunately, I could not, and no one else had an alternative. After much agonizing, Beame reluctantly agreed to sign it—in two places—with a very shaky hand. Then Harvey and I were given a ride in a police car to the home of Judge Irving Saypol, the former U.S. attorney who had prosecuted Julius and Ethel Rosenberg, spies for the Soviet Union. We woke up Judge Saypol and asked him to sign the petition and the stay order to prevent the banks from seizing any city money. At that hour, in his pajamas, he may not have known exactly what he was signing, but we communicated the absolute urgency of getting it done, or risking the unknown for the city. Before the sun was up, the city sent a fleet of police motorcycles to stand by in front of Weil's offices on Fifth Avenue and 59th Street, ready to serve the stay order on all the banks before they opened in the morning. Everyone, including me, thought it was all over. No one could predict the consequences.

Howard Rubenstein, the mayor's public relations advisor, prepared a press release on October 17, 1975, which began: "I have been advised by the Comptroller that the City of New York has insufficient cash on hand to meet debt obligations due today. The financing which was to be made available by the Municipal Assistance Corporation will not be forthcoming because the Teachers Retirement Fund failed to approve its participation in the State Financing Plan. This constitutes the default that we have struggled to avoid. . . ."

Thankfully, neither the motorcycles nor the press release were used. Shanker finally caved to pressure from Governor Hugh Carey and phoned the mayor to tell him the union would buy the bonds. By that time, Shanker was aware of the petition and knew the motorcycle fleet was ready to serve papers on the banks. He also knew he'd be cast as the villain in all the news reports the next day if the city did file for bankruptcy.

Before he knew Shanker had agreed, Beame was meeting in the basement of Gracie Mansion with his key deputies and some leaders of the city council. They were reviewing and approving a detailed plan of what must be done in case of a default. This included paying key city employees (fire, police, hospital, power) in cash, but in a move certain to outrage other big city unions, paying other municipal workers in scrip, notes that could eventually be converted to cash.

The city was "saved," but the same could not be said for Beame's career. He did what he was capable of to win back the trust of those around him. Governor Carey and the governor's close advisor, Lazard Frères investment banker Felix Rohatyn, asked me, Howard Rubenstein, and John Zuccotti to convince Beame to resign. We refused. Beame may not have been a forceful leader, but we felt loyal to him. He had stood up and signed the petition, distasteful as it was.

The mayor asked me to supervise a memo for him that listed everything good he had done, like proposing budget cuts of $1 billion, including $400 million in layoffs. The memo also had some arguably disingenuous "quotes" from the governor, including this gem: "Mayor Beame is a diligent, devoted, and determined leader of the city . . . I have high regard, respect, and admiration for him." A close friend of the former mayor called that "the biggest lie that has ever been told in politics. He didn't think that for one second."

Beame's career was undone by a scathing report in 1977 from the SEC, which came within a stone's throw of accusations of fraud. Among other things, he once said at a press conference that he would personally buy more New York City bonds. The SEC contended that he misled public investors in the offer, sale, and distribution of billions of dollars of the city's municipal securities.

I got into a heated argument with SEC Enforcement Division head Stanley Sporkin over the timing of the mean-spirited report's release. It was sitting on Sporkin's desk in early 1977, ready to go. I pleaded with him to issue the report in February or, at the latest, by March, because it would give the mayor time to explain himself to the public before the Democratic primary in September, where he would be up against New York Congressman Edward Koch, New York Secretary of State Mario Cuomo, and the large-hatted Bella Abzug, a former congresswoman and leader of the women's movement.

By late June, still no report. I was unhappy, and confronted Sporkin. "Stanley, this is really an outrage," I said. "How can you do this? You're in effect handing the election to whoever is running against him. That's not right. You know it's not right. We've been at this now for months."

But Sporkin waited until only a week or two before the primary to issue the report. Koch won the primary and a runoff vote against Cuomo, who ran on the Liberal Party ticket in the general election. Koch prevailed, beating out Cuomo and the Republican candidate, Roy Goodman, a New York state senator who represented Manhattan's Upper East Side for years.

City politics being what they always are, I don't believe the delay was an accident. I don't believe it was in President Carter's interest, because Beame had swung the New York delegation to Carter during the primary season the year before, although Beame's initial "endorsement" of Carter was bizarre, to say the least.

On the day Beame "endorsed" Carter, Howard Rubenstein and I brought Carter to Gracie Mansion. Carter had requested this—he wanted Beame's endorsement for the democratic nomination for president. Carter had no big-city mayor behind him. But Beame wouldn't come downstairs to

Figure 6.2   Mayor Abe Beame, Ira Millstein, and President Jimmy Carter (1976).

meet him. Howard begged him to, and he finally agreed to come down to the meeting. Carter asked multiple times for Beame's endorsement, but the mayor said nothing. He just sat there with his hands folded in front of him. The silences were terribly embarrassing. Then Beame left and went back upstairs, never having said a word. Totally frustrated, Howard suddenly blurted out, "The mayor endorses you." Carter flashed his trademark toothy smile, said, "That's wonderful!" and scooted out.

The next morning, *The New York Times* reported that Beame had endorsed Carter. Nobody knew that the only person at the meeting who had endorsed him was Howard, who assumed his job as the mayor's publicist was now over. But Beame called him to say, "You did the right thing."

Figure 6.3   Ira Millstein poses with Mayor Abe Beame (1976).

Beame was convinced that a friendly president would be a "good thing" for the city.

If left to himself, Beame would probably never have endorsed Carter. He disliked him. Once elected, Carter never did much for the city, despite a letter he signed the night of his nomination listing everything he would do for the city. Many of us felt let down. For the sake of the city, Beame had been key to Carter's nomination. The city deserved more help, and needed it. In any event, once the feisty Ed Koch was elected mayor, Abraham Beame simply disappeared.

The New York City fiscal crisis was among the worst examples of poor corporate governance oversight I have seen. There was utterly no accountability, no checks, and no balances. Just consider the enormous deficit the city operated under and its failure to implement sound accounting practices. Instead of recognizing the city's ever-growing financial problems, city officials buried their heads in the sand and borrowed even more money that they should have known could not be repaid. Except for Epley, the lonely bank lawyer who blew the whistle, the banks were no help. New York City teetered on the brink of bankruptcy, which should be a lesson to everyone on what can happen when there is no system equivalent to corporate governance in place to monitor those we entrust with the public's welfare.

There is also a lesson to be learned from a slumbering board of a major public utility, which put the people and economy of the nation's largest city in peril.

7

LIGHTS OUT

The Con Ed Blackout

On the evening of July 13, 1977, Manhattan went dark. A cascading series of human dysfunction, poor judgment, malfunctioning equipment, and inadequate training at Consolidated Edison, New York's main power utility, coalesced into a massive system collapse that lasted almost twenty-four hours. Even more notable was that, according to the minutes of the first Con Ed board meeting following the blackout, *not a single director* asked tough questions or pressed for information about the disaster beyond those offered in a management presentation, which in retrospect seemed all too brief and superficial.

Had the board been dutifully performing its roles and responsibilities, including providing guidance to and oversight of management, the blackout may have been avoided. This could have included steps such as:

- building a more diverse board consisting of additional directors with industry knowledge, operational experience, and functional expertise in the field of electric service;

- creating an active risk committee responsible for implementing risk management policies based on an analysis of Con Ed's operations; and
- asking management the tough questions, including whether employees were properly trained, what steps management had taken after the 1965 power outage to avoid another blackout, and what emergency systems were in place in the event of system failures to avoid a cascading effect leading to complete darkness.

In our investigation, we found no evidence of any of the foregoing.

As the details of what actually happened that night emerged, the outrage meter of New Yorkers in general and of City Hall in particular moved solidly into the red zone. When Con Ed called the blackout an "act of God," Mayor Abraham Beame raged and accused the utility of "gross negligence." I was working with the mayor as an unpaid advisor on fiscal matters. He asked me to chair a Special Commission of Inquiry into Energy Failures, a four-month effort that resulted in a 336-page report explaining in excruciatingly (especially for Con Ed) granular detail the precipitating events (figure 7.1).

The report's facts and conclusions are instructive as a manual on how *not* to manage, oversee, or monitor a utility that is responsible for the personal and economic welfare of ten million people. It was like opening the instructions for a piece of complicated electronic equipment to find it contained just two words: "Good luck!"

The New York Times

LATE CITY EDITIO

Weather: Partly sunny today; m
tonight. Warm, humid tomorr
Temperature range: today 68..:
yesterday 73-87. Details, page E

20 CENT

NEW YORK, WEDNESDAY, AUGUST 31, 1977

25 cents beyond 50-mile zone from New York City.
Higher in air delivery cities.

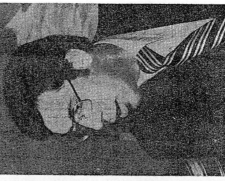

BLACKOUT INQUIRY BEGINS: Ira M. Millstein, left, who heads city-appointed panel investigating July 13 power-failure, conducting opening session yesterday. Edward

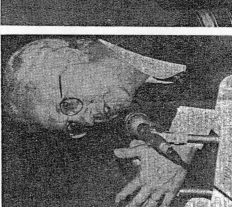

The New York-Times/Paul Hosefos

Hr.Jurith, whose father was in charge of the Con Ed system that night, said his father was too sick to testify and refused to answer commission questions. Page D13.

Figure 7.1 Ira Millstein, Special Commission of Inquiry into Energy Failures chairman, investigates blackout (1977).

At 8:37 p.m. on July 13, an apparent lightning strike on two important Con Ed feeder lines in northern Westchester County caused short circuits that opened two large high-speed circuit breakers. Normally breakers automatically close within seconds, with barely a dip in the lights. But on this evening, the system didn't respond properly and service wasn't restored. One of the feeders had an improperly maintained circuit breaker, and the other couldn't reclose because Con Ed had failed to complete the installation of a reclosing circuit.

With those open circuits, the number 3 nuclear generating plant at Indian Point on the Hudson River, fifty miles north of Manhattan, automatically shut down—a built-in safety process intended to prevent a dangerous overload at the facility. This cut power generation that could have kept the lights on in Manhattan. But restarting a nuclear power plant takes hours.

Like dominoes, more and more circuit breakers opened without reclosing. Remaining feeder lines were dangerously overloaded. Meanwhile, "pilot error" escalated the system meltdown. The Con Ed system operator—the man in charge at the operations center in Manhattan—was unprepared to deal with a crisis of this magnitude. He was flustered, unaware of the basic concepts and complexities behind power system management, and unresponsive to repeated warnings from supervisors to "shed load"—that is, reduce electricity demand by disconnecting various service sectors. Which sectors to close down or black out, in a city as diverse as New York, is a political and practical problem that should have been thoughtfully considered in advance.

But apparently it was not. The decisions were left to a systems operator.

At 8:59 p.m., for example, the senior dispatcher at the Schenectady-based New York Power Pool, which coordinates electricity supply and demand throughout the state, warned the Con Ed system operator that unless he shed load, "you're going to lose everything down there." The Con Ed operator replied: "I'm trying to."

"You're trying to—all you have to do is hit the button to shed it and then we'll worry about it afterwards—but you got to do something . . ." said the senior dispatcher, to which the system operator responded, "Yeah, right. Yeah, fine."

At 9:02 p.m., the system operator called the Power Pool senior dispatcher back and asked for help.

"I can't do nothing," the dispatcher said, "because it's got to come from the lower part of the state, and there's nothing there to help you with. . . . You're going to have to shed load because that's the only way that thing is going to save you. . . ."

"Can you help me?" pleaded the system operator.

"There's no way I can help you, see?"

Manual attempts to shed load didn't work. Why? One possibility the commission considered after examining the load-shedding console and interrogating the system operator, was that he didn't lift the protective covers from the console before trying to depress the buttons. Also, an automatic load-shedding system, designed to limit the extent of the power failure, didn't function as intended.

By 9:36 p.m., the entire Con Ed service area plunged into darkness. And it happened at the worst possible time—in the midst of a brutal summer heat wave, during a spate of

Depression-level unemployment for many of the poor and disadvantaged. At first, most Manhattanites, especially those who survived the 1965 power outage, treated it like a party. Bars poured free drinks. Volunteers served as traffic cops. In Harlem, spontaneous street bonfires and boom-box bursts of soul temporarily turned the area into a kind of street festival.

But then came the vandalism, looting, and arson. The fire department responded to over a thousand fires. Over five hundred police officers were injured and more than four thousand people were arrested. Thieves hot-wired and stole fifty new Pontiacs from a Bronx car dealership and chopped them for parts. In Brooklyn, looters backed their cars up to storefronts and hitched ropes to pull away metal security gates.

I was with the mayor that evening in his private office at City Hall to monitor reports. The police cordoned off Harlem at 125th Street from the rest of the city to contain the chaos. That was largely successful, but one or more felons did manage to break into Brooks Brothers on Madison Avenue in midtown.

Governor Hugh Carey called Beame to say he was sending the National Guard over the George Washington Bridge to control the violence. But Beame was adamantly opposed. He said that if Carey proceeded, he would order the NYPD to block the bridge and prevent the soldiers from entering the city. After a somewhat rancorous "But I'm the one in charge here!" debate, the governor backed off.

The damage totaled $350 million. Our newly formed commission's investigation began immediately. Our investigation included, to name just a few things, inspecting Con Ed generating facilities, conducting interviews and public and private hearings, and sifting through countless documents to diagnose the causes of the blackout. It was four months of work, and I discovered that conducting a public hearing was a learning experience—for me. One of our commissioners, a former prosecutor, had to tell me how to swear in a witness. I learned quickly but sympathized with the Con Ed operator who couldn't push the right button—he was untrained and took the rap for all the others who knew what to do but left him in charge. We went as easy on him as we could, but the facts were there. They left him to play the villain.

Our report, published on December 1, 1977, put the primary blame squarely on Con Ed management. While the blackout illuminated several governance failures at Con Ed, it is clear that, at a minimum, there was little management oversight and excessive risk-taking, with foreseeable consequences. To the extent that there was a restoration plan, it was cobbled together that night, and none of it worked. Personnel in charge of the system weren't properly trained—in fact, Con Ed had no formalized program for selecting and training its system operators. The facilities in the Manhattan control center were obsolete. A significant amount of the generating system in Manhattan malfunctioned or was out of service. Auxiliary pumps to maintain oil pressure in underground cables, which would have sped up recovery, were never installed. Con Ed had removed its remote-control startup system for gas turbines and left the sites unmanned.

Everything that could have gone wrong did go wrong. And management knew—or should have known—about virtually every problem. Both the Federal Power Commission and the New York State Public Service Commission had made extensive recommendations after the 1965 blackout, but Con Ed, we found, had heeded none of them.

Moreover, the Public Service Commission itself never followed up to compel Con Ed to comply, though it was aware that the utility was without a preventive maintenance program in effect *prior* to the blackout—a fact made public in a prior case by Carolyn Brancato, an expert in regulatory economics who served as an expert witness on behalf of the New York state attorney general. Overall, the utility was totally insulated from the kind of accountability one would expect in a private competitive atmosphere. Accountability, it seemed to us, was even more important for an organization responsible for ten million people.

During our investigation, Con Ed behaved strangely. In October, Charles F. Luce, the Con Ed chairman, wrote to me acknowledging that two members of his staff had received requests from the special commission to meet with the Con Ed board. Luce suggested that I write him a letter making the request formal, with the odd comment that it "would be helpful if you would state in your letter as clearly as possible the commission's purpose in seeking to meet with our Board." What on earth would a Special Commission of Inquiry into Energy Failures want to talk about other than the blackout? An analysis of the rate base? An update on capacity? Ultimately, it didn't matter, since the board refused to meet with us (figure 7.2). We were surprised at their refusal, since the board was comprised of some of New York's best.

One of the most alarming discoveries was that Arthur Hauspurg, the Con Ed president and a member of the board, testified before our commission *that subsequent to the power*

City Panel Blasts Con Ed's Report; Management Hit

By STEVE LAWRENCE

A special city commission will show in hearings next week that last month's blackout stemmed from "a management failure, not merely the failure of one system operator" at Consolidated Edison, according to commission counsel Jonathan Rosner.

Rosner charged yesterday that Con Edison has not given "the full picture" of the causes of the July 13 power failure.

Rosner, general counsel to the city's Special Commission of Inquiry into Energy Failures, said that next week's hearings would reveal "some failures not included in Con Edison's report, internal policies and mandated procedures that will evidence a management failure—not merely the failure of one system operator."

Commission Chairman Ira Millstein went out of his way yesterday to rebut a charge by Con Ed Board Chairman Charles Luce that the special commission is engaging in a "political maneuver" by scheduling its first public hearings just before the mayoral primary.

"Not Politically Motivated"

"This is not a politically motivated commission," Millstein said. Luce had turned down a request to appear voluntarily at those hearings because, as he wrote in a letter to the commission two days ago, he considered them "political."

But Con Edison President Arthur Hauspurg said on Wednesday that the utility would comply with any of the commission's "legal subpenas."

Mayor Beame has already called one City Hall press conference to release what he said was a "significant" gap in Con Edison's account of the blackout. The mayor said the special commission had discovered that Con Edison had trouble restarting one of its nuclear power plants while trying to restore power to the city July 14.

Con Edison denied that the nuclear plant's startup problems had anything to do with the blackout or with its problems in restoring power to the city.

And last night the company maintained that it had provided the special commission with "all the documents, tapes and other materials it requested."

Ira Millstein
Chairman of city commission

Con Ed charged that Millstein's allegation regarding a lack of full disclosure "is but another example of the city's policy of saying we will have a fair trial before we hang the defendant."

Hauspurg said Wednesday that a series of human errors in the utility's control center contributed to the blackout. He claimed "the system operator should have taken certain actions sooner than he did."

In the firm's first admission that the blackout was more than just "an act of God," Hauspurg conceded that the system might have recovered from the effects of lightning if it had not been for a succession of other events that he said were "mechanical and human" and that contributed to the total power shutdown.

Figure 7.2 Ira Millstein conducting open session during the blackout inquiry (1977).

failure, the board did not meet in emergency session or take any action concerning or relevant to the power failure. With great reluctance and only under threat of subpoena did Con Ed finally provide us with minutes of the utility's board meetings, and they were heavily expurgated. In a letter to the *New York Times*, which surprised us by criticizing our report, we replied, "We have, of course, no reason to believe that among the portions of the minutes which were deleted by Con Ed are passages which would have portrayed the Trustees as taking an active interest in this matter of grave concern to the general public and, presumably, to Con Ed."

Our report offered several recommendations for institutionalizing a significant degree of management responsibility, including adding three outside directors to the board—appointed by the governor, mayor, and Westchester's county executive—with backgrounds and sufficient staff resources to act independently as a window into Con Ed's board and management. We also urged the Public Service Commission to establish economic performance criteria and economic sanctions ensuring that Con Ed would receive a lower rate of return if it didn't live up to the criteria. "Thus stockholders, and not ratepayers, will be financially penalized for management's mistakes," we concluded. "This happens in private industry and what we are trying to accomplish is to approximate some of the same competitive stimulus for efficiency."

By any measure, with no apparent meaningful oversight or regard for consequences that we could find, this was a star example of management dysfunction, director inertia, and no meaningful corporate governance. And consider this: as far as the commission knew, Con Ed's board did not promptly investigate this catastrophic failure—a voluntary step that a responsible board would have taken to underlie corrective actions—especially for a utility serving millions and a blackout of this scope. Presumably had the board done any of the foregoing, it had a responsibility to report it to the public so greatly harmed, and to the commission.

Unfortunately Con Ed is not the only example of the public being harmed because a board looked the other way. Boards of entities created with the specific purpose of serving the public have far too often ignored their duties as directors, and have failed to provide management oversight, as we will see.

8

SHEDDING LIGHT ON SHADOW GOVERNMENT

This story is about what might happen if government and its entities, and even legislatures, recognized their fiduciary duties to us, the taxpayers. In the same way that we demand an accounting from the private sector of its fiduciary duties to us as investors, government and legislatures could, and should, impose those obligations on themselves.

New York is known for its multitude of public authorities—the hundreds of state and local entities used to raise and spend taxpayer money for public benefit endeavors like mass transit and school construction without the obligation to seek voter approval through a general obligation debt referendum. That, of course, would result in higher taxes, something voters tend not to want. By contrast, public authorities raise their money through the issuance of public debt (bonds and the like), which is then repaid with revenues from the various projects, like bridge and tunnel tolls or train fares. Together, these NYC public authorities are responsible for over $261 billion in state debt, 60 percent of which is issued by state authorities, and incur operating expenses that exceed $41 billion annually.

Certainly many of these endeavors became, and many still are, essential to the way taxpayers live their lives. But the problem is that entities like the Metropolitan Transportation Authority (MTA), the Empire State Development Corporation, the New York State Power Authority, local water, sewer, and resource recovery authorities—and at one point, even something called the Overcoat Development Corporation— historically functioned as a shadow government, kept secret from the view of the taxpayers. Too often, many boards of these public authorities were filled with political cronies of whichever administration appointed them. They played by their own rules and indulged in sweetheart deals, secrecy, fiscal mismanagement, and good old-fashioned corruption. Although these authorities were subject to general statutory reporting requirements, the legislature, the executive branch, and the state comptroller historically exercised minimal enforcement. Without vigilant oversight, public authorities operated with little public accountability or transparency. Our system of public authorities evolved into a hodgepodge of corporations without governance.

The malfeasance list is too long and lurid to describe in detail, but a recent example was in 2003 when three current and former MTA officials were indicted in an $18 million overbilling and bribery scheme, and the authority itself was accused of manipulating finances to justify a controversial fare increase. Then in 2004, New York Assemblyman Richard Brodsky began a broad series of investigations into the state's public authorities. His probes uncovered all sorts of mischief and questionable deals: the New York Thruway Authority's grant of exclusive land-use rights along a section of the Erie Canal for a mere $30,000, and the MTA's attempted sale of the West Side Rail Yard for a figure far below market. Brodsky later found fiscal mismanagement by the Roosevelt Island Operating Corporation, including inadequate long-range planning, the failure to secure potential outside grants, and relying on one-off cash infusions at the expense of long-term income streams.

Brodsky also took on the New York Yankees and the New York City Industrial Development Agency, which floated $3 billion to build the new Yankee Stadium. His investigation revealed secret and ethically questionable deals between the Yankees and the city: publicly funded luxury boxes for city officials, little job creation, and high ticket prices. He also investigated former Congressman John Sweeney for inviting personal guests, lobbyists, and contributors to a ski weekend at the Lake Placid Olympic site, hosted by the Olympic Regional Development Corporation and paid for with $25,000 in public funds by the New York State Power Authority, both of which are state public authorities.

In 2004, Governor George Pataki retained me, pro bono, as an advisor and chair of a committee on public authority corporate governance. Our task was to develop and recommend solutions to ensure effectiveness and transparency in these state entities. In February 2005, the governor formed the New York State Commission on Public Authority Reform, which I chaired. Members of the commission were Peter Clapman, Elizabeth W. Factor, Diana Fortuna, Jane Hoffman, Honorable James P. King, Alan Levine, Louis Lowenstein, John F. McGillicuddy, J. Thomas Roohan, Honorable Jay T. Snyder, Carole E. Stone, and Kathryn S. Wylde.

Our task was to implement the model principles of effective corporate governance that the committee had developed and to recommend policies governing the responsible and transparent disclosure of financial information and guidelines for the conduct of internal and independent audits.

The commission's recommendations spurred legislative action to reform the governance of our public authorities. Working with Brodsky and other members of the commission, we drafted the Public Authorities Accountability Act of 2005, an unprecedented piece of legislation that codified in executive law an independent inspector general, established a new independent budget office for oversight and compliance work, strengthened public reporting and disclosure requirements, and separated the oversight and executive functions of authority boards. In describing the act, Brodsky said, "This is the most fundamental reform of state government in decades. We have begun to bring these Soviet-style bureaucracies under control."

While the Public Authorities Accountability Act brought some much-needed structural changes, it even more importantly established substantive directives to guarantee transparency and responsible oversight. But there was much more to be done. Echoing a key mission in the corporate world, Brodsky and I insisted that New York needed new directives to spell out the importance of ensuring that boards of directors, and the individuals responsible for appointing and designating those directors, understand, acknowledge, and respect the fiduciary duty owed by public authority board members. Again, we worked with the legislature and the executive branch, speaking regularly with Senator Bill

Perkins and those working in Governor David Paterson's office, particularly Peter Kiernan, counsel to Paterson. We reached agreement on the Public Authorities Reform Act of 2009, which Governor Paterson signed into law in December 2009. This new law enacted comprehensive reform to the obligations and duties of public authority board members. For the first time, New York State established the principle of a fiduciary duty owed by directors of public authorities and those with the authority to appoint them.

Employing fiduciary law concepts, we wrote into the Public Authorities Law an explicit fiduciary requirement: Each board member is to act in good faith and with that degree of diligence, care, and skill which an ordinarily prudent person in like position would use under similar circumstances, and ultimately apply independent judgment in the best interest of the authority, its mission, and the public. To ensure that each individual serving as a board member of a public authority understands his or her obligation as a fiduciary, the Public Authorities Law also requires that each director sign an Acknowledgement of Fiduciary Duties and Responsibilities reflecting these obligations. In practical terms, this meant that board members could not appropriately exercise their fiduciary duties if they could be swayed by fear, friendship, or personal gain—all of which too often guided the decision-making of many public authority directors.

When Paterson signed the Public Authorities Reform Act into law, he formed a task force to identify and examine issues associated with the implementation of the act, and to provide policy direction and advice to an empowered independent oversight office. He called it the Authorities Budget Office, which was created by the Act to enforce the new law. Paterson asked me to chair this task force.

We met with the boards of directors of a broad range of the state's public authorities, including the Empire State Development Corporation, NYC Industrial Development Agency, Dormitory Authority of the State of New York, Westchester County Health Hospitals Corporation, Dutchess County Resource Recovery Agency, Power Authority of the State of New York, and New York State Thruway Authority. It was clear in the task force's educational and fact-finding research that many directors were completely unaware of what fiduciary duty meant, and that it applied to them with the force of law behind it. This lack of awareness wasn't indifference, but simply due to the fact that up until that moment, nobody had articulated the concept or explained what it entailed. It was not uncommon for board members to fall back on the excuse that as part-time, unpaid volunteers they could not be expected to exercise the diligence, care, and oversight required by fiduciary duty.

Particularly troublesome in our fact-finding were the accounts of how people who appointed board members to public authority boards tried to influence their decision-making—another given in the pre-reform era. We found the potential for such objectionable activity to be considerable, and urged, among other things, mandated training sessions targeting individuals with the power to appoint. In too many instances we found that board members were surprised to learn that their fiduciary duty is to the public authority that they serve, rather than to the person who appointed them.

One of the most egregious examples of rampant mismanagement and corruption within a public authority was the New York State Theatre Institute (NYSTI). NYSTI was established in 1974 with the mission of providing theater and education programs for the children, youth, and educators of New York State. NYSTI was primarily funded through a direct state budget appropriation, which in fiscal year 2009–2010 was $3,066,000.

Based on information that NYSTI improperly paid for travel of non-NYSTI employees, the New York State Office of the Inspector General began an investigation. The results of the investigation, which included interviewing 32 witnesses, examining approximately 50,000 documents obtained from NYSTI, and reviewing more than 30,000 of NYSTI's financial transactions, was alarming. According to an April 2010 report by the inspector general, NYSTI, under the direction of Producing Director Patricia Snyder, "failed to recognize NYSTI's existence as a public entity subject to the state's ethics rules." The inspector general determined that NYSTI's board of directors permitted Snyder, over a long period, to "exercise virtually unfettered control and final decision-making authority over nearly every aspect of NYSTI's activities, allowing Snyder to use her authority to engage in a pattern of activities which benefited herself and members of her family in contravention of the state Public Officers Law." Snyder had routinely hired members of her immediate family for NYSTI productions, disregarding state prohibitions on conflicts of interest. Snyder's son and his company were selected at least 182 times for NYSTI productions and received benefits of more than $239,350.

Snyder also ignored state restrictions on self-dealing and executed a number of questionable agreements that resulted in benefits to herself of more than $88,000 in addition to her salary.

Throughout Snyder's reign, there were virtually no internal fiscal controls to provide oversight. The general sentiment at NYSTI seemed to be, as articulated by its business manager: "All I can say is, I don't make decisions. If Patricia hands me things and tells me to pay for it, I pay for it." According to the inspector general's report, even NYSTI's independent financial auditor, a certified public accountant, had very limited knowledge of NYSTI's frequent use of a bank account from which numerous improper expenditures were made.

In a remarkably swift and consequential move, and following the recommendation of the Authorities Budget Office, which found that NYSTI's directors failed to perform their duties in good faith, Paterson demanded the resignation of the entire board of directors of the NYSTI in May 2010, based on a "persistent pattern of neglect in the performance of its duties and fiduciary obligations." Ultimately, NYSTI was dissolved and its statutory authority repealed. What we created was working.

Currently under the direction of Governor Andrew Cuomo, I still chair the task force today, frequently providing guidance, when asked, to the Authorities Budget Office on the implementation of the Public Authorities Reform Act. During the past five years, the Authorities Budget Office has made strides in uncovering and demanding public accountability from those individuals who abuse the system. Though short on staff and shamefully underfunded, the Authorities Budget Office, under the stewardship of David Kidera, still holds public authorities accountable for their disclosure obligations and devotes its resources to investigating public authority abuses.

Institutions as disparate as sovereign wealth funds and legislatures could learn from an explicit acknowledgment of fiduciary duties, related training, and better transparency. The effects of transparency and greater accountability should never be underestimated. Fiduciary duties should be articulated and enforced throughout government and all public entities.

Often the problem is systemic, so its exposure is useful in any event. We aren't so naive as to think that rigid new policy guidelines, aggressive reeducation, or better oversight would solve all problems. But as in the corporate world, while good governance is no guarantee of improved performance, it is at least far more likely to prevent bad performance.

I hope that my work with the state of New York stands as a beacon, but I have no illusions that elected officials will endorse this concept easily or spread its applicability. That is unless we who elect them, pressure them, or elect officials like Assemblyman Brodsky, Governor Pataki, and Governor Paterson.

Some boards subject to scrutiny by the government because of their mission have recognized the need to implement effective corporate governance before it becomes too late. Such has been the case with a not-for-profit organization I became involved with, which is in the headlines today for all the wrong reasons.

9

PLANNED PARENTHOOD: A CORPORATE
GOVERNANCE SUCCESS STORY

Not-for-profit organizations (NFPs) have good and bad governance moments, as do all public and private corporations. But because NPFs think of themselves as performing some social good, they often overlook their governance failings, which too often lead to unwelcome consequences. Sometimes it's hubris, other times simply inattention. What I found missing in many NFPs were generally applicable good governance practices, which could be adapted to even "do-gooder" organizations. Using our general governance expertise, my firm has assisted many NFPs over the years. Planned Parenthood stands out as one that welcomed our assistance and took our recommendations to heart.

Publicly held corporations hold no monopoly on bad management or poor board oversight. In 1995, William Aramony, the longtime head of The United Way, was convicted of diverting $1.2 million of the foundation's funds for personal benefit. His infamous deeds included buying a $450,000 condo for his seventeen-year-old girlfriend (Aramony was fifty-nine at the time). Then there was Larry

Jones, founder of Feed the Children, who was in the headlines for years over alleged financial impropriety and mismanagement, who finally settled a wrongful termination
suit by the board in 2011. And in Prince George's County,
Maryland, the county executive was indicted on conspiracy,
extortion, and bribery charges. The list goes on.

Planned Parenthood Federation of America, on the other
hand, provides an example of a board that takes its responsibilities seriously, overseeing management and evaluating
its own governance structure to head off problems before it
becomes too late.

My own involvement in the nonprofit dustup was as the
advisor to a three-person board committee of Planned Parenthood. Weil had done some work for Planned Parenthood
in the early 1990s and I had once met Eve Paul, the organization's vice president and general counsel, at a fundraiser in
Manhattan.

In April 1995 I received an inquiry from Thomas Borman,
a Minnesota attorney who was on the Planned Parenthood
board. He wanted Weil to advise the board regarding concerns with Pamela Maraldo, the highly compensated federation president, who had joined the organization two years
before from the National League for Nursing, a Washington,
DC–based nonprofit.

Planned Parenthood retained Weil and we soon learned
that the board had some serious concerns about Maraldo's
performance. The board had no confidence in her abilities
to represent the organization. For example, on television,
in marked contrast to her poised, put-together predecessor, Maraldo was uncomfortable and uneasy, fidgeting and

coming out with lines like "It's a the-whole-is-greater-than-the-sum-of-the-parts kind of thing."

Board confidence in Maraldo's leadership had eroded beyond recovery. Some members of the board and some within the organization feared that Maraldo was abandoning Planned Parenthood's original focus on reproductive health services and was reinventing the organization to offer general medical services, in competition with local HMOs. Media coverage that focused on Maraldo's controversial "reinvention" plan did not help.

Alexander Sanger, executive director of Planned Parenthood of New York City and the grandson of Margaret Sanger, the founder of Planned Parenthood, told *The New York Times* in the summer of 1995, "Maybe we could market ourselves better, as some people suggested, if every clinic offered the same services, looked the same, and was open the same hours. It works for McDonald's. But that's not the history of this organization."

I quickly realized that what I started at General Motors—creating an active board to provide management oversight and, when necessary, replace management—should not be limited to publicly held corporations. Rather, it was just as important, if not more so, for boards of NFPs to monitor, evaluate, and hold members of management accountable for their actions. The public, and donors of course, depend on these NFPs to operate with effective governance structures that will be responsible to supporters and best serve the organizations' needs. I counseled the Planned Parenthood board on its fiduciary duties, including duty of care, and on the importance of overseeing management. The board knew that, while it was a difficult decision to make, the right thing for Planned Parenthood was for Maraldo to leave. The board decided to address the problem in a timely way, before it became a crisis.

The board negotiated an exit for Maraldo—never an easy process even in the best of circumstances, which this was not. Maraldo resigned in July 1995. The media quickly picked up the story, attributing the departure to a failure to "muster a vote of confidence" from the Planned Parenthood board of directors. In fact, the board demonstrated the wisdom of an NFP's responsibility to oversee management in order to protect the integrity of the organization.

But Weil's work for Planned Parenthood wasn't done. The organization retained us again in 2006 to advise on the organization's bylaws and board composition.

Planned Parenthood was unique in that it operated as a federation, with each affiliate retaining control of its own internal affairs. Operating in every state, the network of 120 affiliates provided healthcare to over three million people and an education program that reached 1.5 million. Additionally, Planned Parenthood ran more than 860 local health centers across the United States.

Planned Parenthood operated as a membership organization and was governed by a board of directors nominated by the national nominating committee (NNC). The NNC was a committee of the membership, rather than the board, and was comprised of eight to eleven members. At least five NNC members were to be Planned Parenthood directors and three members were to be designated by the Planned Parenthood regions.

Planned Parenthood's board began to realize that its federated model of independent affiliates was inefficient for many reasons. As Planned Parenthood continued to expand, considerable time and energy was expended communicating with its growing number of affiliates, without any clear processes in place. Too often the affiliates were operating independent of one another, duplicating efforts. The result was lost opportunities for collaboration, shared resources, and economies of scale. Fundraising efforts by affiliates and the national office were often in direct competition. Many affiliates had limited or no capacity to be effective in the all-important public policy arena, and had been unable to efficiently address critical regulatory, legislative, and reimbursement issues.

Additionally, the environment in which nonprofits were operating had been dramatically changing. Since the passage of the Sarbanes-Oxley Act of 2002, nonprofits and their boards were increasingly under heightened scrutiny from Congress, state attorneys general, donors, potential donors, and the media. This environment and the inefficiencies of Planned Parenthood's federated system contributed to its decision to retain Weil to assess the effectiveness of its governance structure and processes.

Weil undertook a comprehensive analysis and wrote detailed recommendations covering the entire scope of the organization's governance procedures. We sought to create a strategic organizational plan that would provide the foundation for a strong national organization where affiliates worked collaboratively toward mutual goals. This required a business model that balanced affiliate autonomy with standardized best practices and centralization of economic activities to realize economies of scale.

As always, the devil is in the details. So we carefully dissected the organization's skeletal structure—its bylaws. We interviewed key members of the organization, including Planned Parenthood's president, Cecile Richards, members of the board of directors, and members of the NNC, to learn more details. The board members and Cecile were open and cooperative, helping us analyze the possible shortfalls in the organization's structure. We all agreed that the bylaws were overly complex and needed to be consolidated, simplified, rearranged, and updated for ease of reference and to reflect what the "new" organization would look like. Without that extensive overhaul of the bylaws, no larger changes could happen.

For one thing, there was no clear statement that Planned Parenthood was a membership organization. We needed to clarify that the NNC, for instance, was responsible for membership matters unrelated to those of regular board committees. The solution was to create a new section of the bylaws (Article VI), which spelled out the duties of the NNC and established an "Affiliate Chief Executive" title to give the regional affiliates a more authoritative role in nominating candidates for NNC or board positions.

Because a small board is generally more efficient than a large one, we proposed changing the size to a range of twenty-five to thirty-one, instead of thirty-two. This reflected the common practice of many corporations that have bylaws designating a range of board size. This provides flexibility and helps boards avoid situations in which they might not be in compliance with their bylaws because of the unexpected departure of one or more directors.

We eliminated the practice of ceding a certain number of board seats to other entities. For several years, for example, a seat had always been reserved for a representative of the Guttmacher Institute, an organization that provides research and public education on reproductive health matters on a global basis. Now Planned Parenthood could cast a broader net for directors who had the qualifications consistent with best practices and avoid "constituent" directors and the potential for conflicted loyalties.

Because the original bylaws were unclear on the process of electing the chairperson, we clarified that the chair should be elected by the membership at the annual membership meeting, following his or her nomination by the NNC and ratification by the board. We eliminated a requirement to include additional nondirector members on every board committee. This not only increased efficiency but also eliminated the possibility of subjecting nonboard members to unanticipated fiduciary duties that would restrict the board's ability to delegate certain tasks to that committee.

To give the board more flexibility, we authorized it to create new board committees (in addition to standing committees) as necessary to carry out whatever specific roles were necessary. To act on urgent board matters, we simplified the makeup of the executive committee from an unwieldy mix of national and regional officials to one of just the officers and three other directors recommended by the chairperson and approved by the board.

· 177 ·

Since it was more and more common for not-for-profit organizations to obtain Directors and Officers indemnification insurance that encouraged involvement without undue concern about financial risk, we believed the board should have the authority to decide whether it was prudent for Planned Parenthood to obtain such coverage, and therefore revised the bylaws accordingly to grant such rights.

We used our experiences with all types of corporations to counsel Planned Parenthood and suggested changes to the board that would enable them to govern effectively and efficiently. It was gratifying to watch advice based on good governance in the for-profit world being ingested and then practiced by an established NFP.

It was the most inclusive, top-to-bottom governance reorganization I can remember, and one that I am extremely proud of to this day. Planned Parenthood recognized our contributions to the organization and honored Weil with the Corporate Leadership Award for "invaluable legal advice that led to significant changes" in Planned Parenthood's governance structure.

Planned Parenthood added NFPs to the list of major and minor publicly held corporations, governments, and public authorities that demonstrated a need for setting a new agenda for governing themselves. It is to that new agenda that I now turn.

CONCLUSION

In Search of the Activist Director

"We cannot solve our problems with the same thinking we used when we created them."

—Albert Einstein

In this, the concluding chapter, I offer my prescriptions to halt backsliding corporate governance, a regress enabled by a mutated capital markets structure, where too many push their own short-term agendas and imperil the growth of corporations and individual portfolios. These agendas are not in the best interest of shareholders or the economy.

The prescriptions I lay out in this chapter focus on a new type of director—a director who recognizes the imperative need for change. Directors, and value-driven shareholders who invest in the long-term future of the corporation, accept responsibility for selecting, retaining, and motivating management through the right incentives, and they want to, and are able to, partner with management to do what is in the best interests of the future of the corporation. That focus is missing today. I will urge that directors be chosen with the same care and diligence as is the case with choosing the CEO.

Throughout this book, we have charted the history of corporate governance in America to discover how we ended up where we are today. A relatively simple capital market structure evolved to one of extraordinary complexity. More often than not, I found that boards of directors didn't change their thinking to stay in step with the changing capital market structure. Boards have the same mindset they did decades ago, when the American economy was flourishing and there was little foreign competition. Back then, boards could remain relatively passive and entrust their managers to grow the corporation.

Today the mantra most common in corporate America is still this: "Boards don't manage, they just oversee." Far too many directors take that hands-off approach; they check the legal compliance boxes and otherwise limit their involvement. The future of the corporation—strategy—is left to management.

This mantra must change. Some argue that change is unnecessary—that developed capital market systems, including corporations, will adjust and eventually correct themselves. I disagree. Yes, markets may self-correct, but only in the long term. In the meantime, the livelihoods of shareholders, employees, customers, and so many others are at risk.

A director—one who recognizes the need for change and accepts my recipe in this chapter for active partnership with management—is not a cure-all for everything wrong in our economy. There is no single solution to the myopia of short-term capital markets. Economists like Joseph Stiglitz, in *Rewriting the Rules of the American Economy*, have theorized how we can incent long-term corporate growth, perhaps through the issuance of loyalty shares or new financial transaction taxes. But boards must face the capital market for what it is today, not what it was, and think about what it may become.

The corporation is the key organizational structure that forms the core of our economy. I believe in boards that safeguard the best interests of the corporation as a whole, and recognize that they are operating in, and confronting, the new capital market.

My prescription is straightforward. It requires a reset of basic values and responsibilities in corporate America. Those whose short-term wealth gains are threatened will ridicule it. But it will be welcomed, I believe, by directors and shareholders who want to ensure the future of their corporate wards.

I don't suggest more intervention by regulators or so-called experts. The solution I propose is more difficult. It is to create a new breed of activist director, one who is conscious of the effects of decision-making, who will drill deeply into a corporation's financials and culture, who will not shrink from confrontation, who will ask tough questions of the CEO when he or she veers off course or when the numbers include unexpected special write-downs.

We need directors who do not miss board meetings and who, on their own time, visit the factory floors to ask workers what could be done to improve morale and productivity. We need directors on the all-important compensation committee who make sure the boss is paid well but not *too* well; and who listen but resist pressure from shareholders with self-serving agendas, or from proxy advisors, the media, and the gratuitous advice of those who impose one-size-fits-all compliance solutions to governance practice.

Most important, we need directors who reject the "nose in, fingers out" (NIFO) attitude that prevails in too many boards—the idea that it is only the CEO who is in charge of the corporation's future.

This director template holds the best hope for leaving short-termism behind. This director serves as an aspirational model for all those who care about their corporation. This template includes guidelines for the performance of directors themselves, and for adding to or replacing board members. Institutional investors and hedge fund shareholders who want to add future value to their holdings through proxy voting for directors should strive to fill boards with activist directors. Academics and the rest of us who depend on corporations should be vocal supporters. I am proposing that the whole corporate community adopt the mindset of an *activist director* who knows his legal mandate and has no qualms executing it aggressively.

EXISTING LAW AND THE ACTIVIST DIRECTOR

More public companies are incorporated in Delaware than in any other state. That's because Delaware's statutory and case law is more predictable and settled. In Delaware, the corporation can conduct its business in any way it so chooses, *as long as* directors act on an informed basis, in good faith, and in the honest belief that the action taken is in the best interests of the company.

This "business judgment rule" means that a court in Delaware—or, for that matter, in any state jurisdiction—is hesitant to substitute its judgment for a board's when the board has exercised its duties of care and loyalty and has acted in good faith, following a reasoned, prudent process in making decisions. In these situations, lawsuits challenging a particular board action, or a decision to take no action, will be dismissed, protecting directors from any personal liability even if the decision may have been questionable.

One of the most important precedents upholding this standard came in June 2006. Delaware's highest court affirmed a lower court determination that Walt Disney directors did not breach their fiduciary duties in the hiring and messy firing of Michael Ovitz or in the handling of his arguably outrageous $140 million termination package—which *New York* magazine calculated to be more than $300,000 a day for his 454 days as president. Disney had brought in the Hollywood superagent to run the company, but the move failed spectacularly. It was, to many, the worst mismanagement decision of all time. But despite this, the court backed Disney's board, not the shareholders who were suing, because in the court's view the board had acted in good faith.

Delaware law, which is followed by many other states, is based on the long-standing principle that the board of directors has the *sole authority* to manage the company, even though in day-to-day operations they delegate that function to management. The legal precedents flow from both the

Delaware General Corporation Law (DGCL) and judicial interpretations of statutory law. The DGCL emphasizes a board-centric approach to corporate governance and supports my vision of the activist director.

While not spelled out in the DGCL, responsibilities of the board under case law typically include, among other things, oversight over whether the company is properly managed; the selection, compensation, and (if needed) removal of a CEO; reviewing and approving the company's financial objectives and major corporate plans and actions; planning for CEO succession; and oversight of auditing, risk assessment, disclosure, and compliance matters. In short, there is more than ample case law to support my proposal that directors are empowered to actively participate in management decisions.

It is time to modernize, shuck the NIFO straightjacket, and spur passive directors to their responsibilities—the law is behind them.

Of course boards are also influenced by mandates from federal law. What this means for directors, as articulated by the outstanding scholar and former Chief of the Delaware Supreme Court, Justice Norman Veasey, is "the federal securities regulatory regime is a force in influencing the internal affairs of corporations." Almost anytime the United States meets a financial crisis, Congress reacts and enacts more regulations, which are adopted by the Securities and Exchange Commission. The SEC was created in the aftermath of the 1929 market crash to regulate the financial community and any public company and its board whose securities are publicly traded.

In response to the Enron and WorldCom scandals of the early 2000s, Congress passed the Sarbanes-Oxley Act of 2002 to overhaul the financial practices of public corporations by focusing on the independence of the audit committee and external auditors. Sarbanes-Oxley, arranged into eleven titles, established a Public Company Accounting Oversight Board; required that audit committees be composed solely of independent directors; implemented CEO and CFO certification requirements for company financial reports; and prohibited personal loans to executives and directors.

Less than ten years later, following the 2008 financial meltdown, public corporations and their directors were subject to more federal law through the Dodd-Frank Wall Street Reform and Consumer Protection Act of 2010. Corporate governance–related requirements under Dodd-Frank mandate disclosing in annual proxy statements the rationale for separating or combining the chairman and CEO positions, "say on pay" rules for shareholders on compensating executives, and prohibiting member brokers from voting customer shares in certain situations. And it's not over. More rules under Dodd-Frank are still to come.

The NYSE and NASDAQ also impose requirements on directors of public corporations that have securities listed on these exchanges. These include periodic reporting requirements, director qualification standards, director certification requirements, and independence standards.

The point is that nothing in all of these interventions prevents directors from assuming the responsibilities I prescribe. If anything, they underscore director responsibilities.

Overwhelmed by a flood of new requirements, boards are spending more and more of their time trying not to run afoul of the rules. Director attention has shifted priorities from managing the affairs of the corporation—corporate strategy, growth, and performance—to "compliance," a necessary but not sufficient responsibility for the activist director.

In my construct of the importance of board attention to strategy, much of this "compliance" work should occur with the general counsel and relevant board committees, leaving the board, as a whole, free to map the strategy of the corporation.

Besides navigating complex laws, directors are coping with the growing influence of proxy advisors. While it is not mandatory, in the legal sense, directors often believe that they can blindly adhere to proxy advisor corporate governance policies, or that, following their advice, boards will immunize themselves and their voting decisions. In either case, the proxy advisors free boards from thinking on their own.

But examine the advice of the advisors: guidelines that are applied wholesale to every public corporation, without scrutinizing each corporation's circumstances. And these advisors are people who were rarely, if ever, in the relevant corporation's boardroom. If corporations don't adopt these wholesale policies, which in essence have become "mandates" rather than guidelines, the proxy advisors may recommend against voting for directors in the next election.

Directors themselves, and their value-driven shareholders using their voices and proxy votes, ought to find and install the kind of directors I call for. I am not advocating that a board operationally run the corporation—that's management's job. Rather, I seek an activist board that is knowledgeable, thinks independently, and is interested enough to *partner* with management in designing the corporation's future, which management can then execute.

HOW TO CREATE ACTIVIST DIRECTORS

First the board must accept responsibility for identifying, screening, and nominating directors. The board presents the slate to shareholders for a vote. With the rise of shareholder proxy access proposals, perhaps directors will take into consideration shareholder suggestions for director nominations. How this proxy access will play out is still too early to predict. In today's practice, it is too often the CEO who dominates this process, and the newly selected directors may not be sufficiently independent to stand against the CEO when they have to.

This must change. Nominating and corporate governance committees are entrusted with identifying and interviewing those qualified to serve as directors and then recommending candidates for nomination. Of course, the CEO is to be consulted, but should not be controlling. It is the task of the nominating and corporate governance committee to devise the search process.

I have seen very few existing examples of nominating and corporate governance committees who ask the right questions while searching for directors. An exception: private equity firms, which generally have a sound understanding of how to select effective boards for their portfolio companies.

The equity firm owner knows its objectives and its short-term and long-term strategies. It picks and places directors with the skills necessary to achieve those goals. The firm carefully and thoughtfully structures the board to ensure that its directors are all of a like mind and possess the skills to carry out the company's mission. They compensate their chosen directors commensurate with the expectation that they have a job to perform. It is unsurprising that private equity funds still outperform public equities, including the S&P 500, over the long term.

So why can't a public company follow suit? There are differences between a private equity firm and a public corporation, certainly. While private equity firm directors are doing what is best for a single owner, public corporation directors must cater to a heterogeneous, often vocal, shareholder base with competing interests. This just means the board must balance these multiple needs and model for itself a "single owner" whose goal is the future success of the corporation, and then act accordingly—a tricky proposition, to be sure.

The challenge to public corporations is that many of their directors and shareholders have minimal experience interviewing board candidates and struggle with the questions to ask that will predict whether the candidate will be a good fit. Human resources officers and outside consultants can be useful resources to help formulate director interview questions.

This will be new territory for boards in selecting directors, but it's the starting point to change board DNA. It will take strong leadership at the board level, similar to what we saw in John Smale at General Motors, for this to happen. It is critical for directors to begin with a clear understanding of the company's mission to identify the desired skill sets and behaviors of current and potential board members. Candidates will be tested in intensive face-to-face interviews. As value-driven shareholders propose directors or vote their proxies, they should apply the same standards. If this is impracticable, then, at the least, shareholders should assure that the board has adopted this approach.

I propose guiding principles for director interviewing. It's critical to develop a list of company-specific, probing interview questions that will test whether the potential director affirmatively understands and embraces the need for change as our capital markets evolve, wants to do the right thing (and *can* do the right thing even when it is easier not to), questions management strategies and asks probing questions, and thinks independently.

Some of the questions I enumerate are directed to persons who are, or have been, directors but appropriately modified, they apply to any potential director.

THE RIGHT THING

What is the "right thing"? There's no one answer, but for guidance, I go back to the work of Adam Smith, who prior to his seminal *Wealth of Nations* treatise, was a professor of moral philosophy at Glasgow University. According to Smith, as elaborated in his book *The Theory of Moral Sentiments* (1759), the people who inhabited the competitive market are expected to have the virtues of "prudence, justice, and beneficence," . . . "temperance, decency, modesty, and moderation," and should be "scrupulous . . . never either to hurt or offend." This was his moral philosophy and was a foundation for the market theory later articulated in *Wealth of Nations*. Smith understood the importance of ethics in business—he knew that ethical behavior was vital to the survival of free markets.

But Smith was a pragmatist. He saw three visions of society. The first was the model society we should strive for. It was made up of prudent, reasonable, rational people who did no harm. The second was a society where people were neither universally good nor bad. They were governed by trade-offs—I won't hurt you if you don't hurt me, or even, I won't do this because you could punish me. The trade-offs created a manageable society. Smith's third view of society was one plagued with perpetual injustice. It was a world that Smith predicted could not survive—the people would revolt. This is the risk we face if we let greed and self-interest perpetuate. For the world of governance, I choose the second pragmatic vision—sufficient to create a functioning market. Even in this model, Smith depended on the power of individual ethics and, I believe, wound up with "do the right thing."

Adhering to this today means directors must put themselves in the place of others who are affected by their decisions, conscientiously considering the right thing to do, no matter the pressures exerted by management, shareholders, proxy advisors, the media, and the like, and then actually doing it. Directors are the navigators, and they should be the moral compass of the corporation.

The corporate governance failures that I have detailed largely occurred because the boards did not display temperance, prudence, and beneficence. Had directors put themselves in the shoes of their shareholders, customers, and employees, would they have made the same decisions? Would they have stayed passive while management had free reign? Would boards have turned away when the financial institutions they were entrusted to govern sold mortgage-backed securities and collateralized debt obligations to individuals who predictably would not be able to repay the loans? What if they had been the ones purchasing the loans? Would a board not question management about the safety of products if they thought more about their loved ones using those products? I wonder whether Drexel would still exist if the board of directors had questioned Michael Milken instead of silently reaping the benefits of his deceptive practices. Could New York City have avoided a financial crisis due to reckless spending and borrowing, putting at risk the welfare of its residents, if banks, regulators, and state officials had set off the alarms? Would a director cave to a self-interested activist seeking a stock market bump if he thought it was not in the best interest of the corporation as a whole?

I think not.

FINDING THE "RIGHT THING" ACTIVIST DIRECTOR

Considering the characteristics Smith envisioned, the next question is, how? How do we evaluate directors to determine whether they will do the right thing for the corporation?

SOME GENERIC QUESTIONS

It is by asking the right questions, it is by digging deep to understand the values of the candidate, it is by a director placing himself where a shareholder stands and asking whether he would trust the candidate to do the right thing. And it is by ensuring that the candidate's beliefs are aligned with those of the board and the corporation. This means that the candidate should not only believe in what the corporation is doing, the services and products it is providing, but also agree with the board's vision for the future. Co-opted from various C-suite behavior interview templates, here are examples of questions that will unearth a candidate's ability to do what is right, rather than what is easy. The questions should be adapted to the experience of the candidate and the needs of the corporation.

- Have you ever had to defend a decision you made as a director even though other influential people were opposed to your decision?
- There are times when members of management, shareholders, or proxy advisors may try to exert pressure on directors for a certain outcome. Have you encountered such a situation? How did you react?
- Have you ever served on a board where certain board members were not, in your opinion, doing what was in the best interests of the corporation as a whole? What did you do?

- Tell me about a time when you strongly disagreed with someone and how it resolved.
- How would you handle a situation where there is pressure to achieve short-term quarterly results at the risk of jeopardizing long-term performance? Have you come across this situation before?
- Have you ever introduced a new idea or policy to the boards you serve on? Did you meet any resistance when trying to implement the new idea or policy? How did you cope with it?
- People make mistakes and sometimes do things that turn out differently than hoped for. Has this happened to you? What happened?
- While serving on boards, what steps do you go through to ensure that your decisions are in the best interests of the corporation?
- What types of decisions do you find the most difficult to make as a director and why?
- When have you gone above and beyond to get a job done?

I wonder whether the directors of the New York State Theatre Institute were screened with similar questions. The board failed to understand its roles and responsibilities, like providing effective oversight when the producing director acted in her personal, rather than the organization's, best interests. Had the directors exercised the fortitude to perform their fiduciary obligations, perhaps the organization, and the board, would still be operating for the public's benefit.

SOME EXECUTIVE COMPENSATION QUESTIONS

Another way to vet a candidate's moral compass is to ask him or her about executive compensation.

A director who puts him- or herself in the shoes of the corporation's shareholders or employees would reject compensation schemes that have no reasonable relationship to performance—simply because compensation consultants gave the green light for the compensation package, or because peer companies have similar compensation schemes. Consider the outsized levels we often see today, where CEO compensation is strongly tied to short-term results and pay is wildly disproportionate to the median employee salary.

Would the candidate consider what is equitable when determining what management should be paid? Would the candidate stand up to the CEO and reduce the CEO's compensation, if needed? If the answers to these questions are no, the candidate cannot be right for the job. Here are questions that predict how a candidate will approach executive compensation decisions while on the current board, based on prior experiences:

- What role have you played on other boards when determining executive compensation?
- What process did you follow to ensure that the compensation was fair?
- What types of internal and external pressures have you faced as a director while determining executive compensation? How did you cope with such pressures?

- Have you ever had to reduce a management member's compensation? If so, why?
- While serving on past boards, what role did proxy advisor policies play when making executive compensation decisions?

SOME INTEREST QUESTIONS

As obvious as it might seem, it is critical to select directors who are *actually interested in what the company does.* There are too many directors who join boards just to build their resumes. If it is a prestigious company, that is enough. If it provides networking opportunities, that is enough. It doesn't matter what the business is.

Why does the candidate want to serve on this specific board? Why is the candidate interested in the company's business? What makes the corporation's mission meaningful? Why would being on this particular board be fun? Has the candidate served on boards in a similar industry? What interests the candidate specifically about this industry? If the candidate isn't interested in the business, then board service is simply a chore.

SOME SKILLS AND EXPERIENCE QUESTIONS

The board must collectively have the right skills and experiences to carry out its responsibilities effectively. Each director candidate must be evaluated against the backdrop of the existing board and what the board will look like in years to come. This requires not only understanding what skills and expertise the candidate has to offer, but also what skills the current board has—and what skills it lacks. Director selection should be holistic. Each director is just one piece of the puzzle. Does the board, as a whole, have the right skills and experiences to do its job?

Optimal board composition—the best mix of skills and experience—will depend on many company-specific factors, including the industry, size, geographic scope, and stage of company development. For example, directors at financial institutions may need more than one financial expert on the board even though the NYSE requires only one financial expert on the audit committee. Boards of healthcare organizations should probably have more than one director who understands the unique compliance requirements to which the industry is subject.

The board should take a short-term and long-term view when evaluating the current board composition. For example, even if there is a financial expert on the board today, perhaps the individual will retire in the next few years, leaving a vacancy on the board. And if the company strategy in the next few years includes expanding to a different industry, the board should consider whether it would be wise to have an expert in such industry. Boards ought to self-evaluate annually, and incorporate this to ensure that the board has the optimal skills to lead the company based on its current and future strategies.

If a corporation has a diverse board of directors, the board will effectively delegate certain matters—especially compliance-related matters—to its board committees while maintaining oversight responsibility. This would allow the board to shift from spending the majority of its time dealing with compliance issues to managing the affairs of the corporation. But this can work only if the board has the right directors.

SOME TIME AND COMMITMENT QUESTIONS

When evaluating director candidates, it is essential to select directors who have time to do the job. I don't believe in arbitrary proxy advisor policies that recommend voting against directors who sit on a certain number of other public company boards. This is another example of proxy advisor guidelines being applied wholesale to every public corporation. Every board must determine what time commitment it requires from each director. Questions that can uncover how much time a candidate is willing to devote are these:

- How much time do you typically spend on other boards?
- How much time each month can you commit to this board?
- What are some examples of your having to set priorities and multitask?
- Have you had scheduling conflicts in the past with your full-time job and the boards you serve on? How do you resolve these conflicts?
- What other obligations do you have?

SOME ATTITUDE QUESTIONS

How do the candidates answer these questions? Are they passive? Do they ask the tough questions? If so, could they be trusted to question management when necessary? Are the candidates truly interested in finding the right board based on their background, expertise, and interests? Do the candidates want to know about the board's culture and the role the board plays within the corporation? What role do they see for themselves? Will they be activist directors? Change agents? Or directors who won't ruffle any feathers? Understanding candidates' motivations requires in-depth face-to-face conversations and asking the right questions.

SOME BOARD-INCENTIVE QUESTIONS

How do we incent this new breed of directors to *act*, when passively monitoring management is considerably easier? Look again at the model of private equity. These firms tend to link director compensation to company performance, incenting directors to active involvement. Director compensation is aligned with management compensation, not in absolute amounts, but in approach.

Today, public corporation directors have little motivation to do anything but show up. This means simply attending an average of eight board meetings a year, spending fewer than five hours per week per board, and complying with the bare minimum of the law.

We should recognize and reward activist directors who avoid short-term goals and focus on long-term growth. The median pay for public company directors was approximately $235,000 in 2014—the median pay for an S&P 500 CEO was $10.3 million. Why? How can we ask directors to be activists, partnering with management, if we don't compensate them accordingly?

Boards of directors ought to thoughtfully develop compensation policies that provide competitive compensation to attract and retain talented directors and motivate directors to focus on the long-term value creation of the corporation. I want to emphasize *long-term* here, not short-term upticks in stock price. Most public company outside directors are paid with a mix of cash and company stock. The equity portion is often restricted or deferred until the director retires from the board—but is paid out irrespective of company performance.

I think this is a problem. To encourage directors to focus on the long-term performance of the corporation, their compensation must align with metrics that directly affect long-term value creation. Compensation objectives should reward personal productivity and foster a long-term vision for the corporation. This philosophy should already be familiar to directors—it is how they should be structuring management compensation policies. I simply ask that the board apply this to themselves. It's not selfish—it's realistic.

Of course I recognize that sanctioning an increase in director compensation invites abuse-of-power criticism, since directors are responsible for evaluating their own performance and setting their own compensation. But transparent disclosure of director compensation policies, the power of shareholders to vote against directors, and selecting only those directors (including by asking the right questions during interviews) who want to do the right thing mitigate this risk. To be clear, I am not encouraging a director compensation approach equal to the outrageous levels we now see in some CEO pay, but rather reasonable amounts that give directors the performance–related incentive to focus on long-term corporate performance.

These questions are simply guidelines to be adapted, depending on whether they are applied to evaluate existing board members or potential candidates, and of course to the context of each individual corporation.

ULTIMATELY "PARTNERING"

I mentioned that the goal of the activist director is "partnering" with management. What I mean is working with management on the strategy for the future. Not rubber-stamping or tinkering with management's obligation to present a strategy. But questioning every part of it, based on the director's expertise, the time he or she has spent understanding the corporation's operations and its competitive context, his or her knowledge of what customers and suppliers expect, the value and importance of the corporation's reputation, and the impact of the strategy on that reputation. The activist director must evaluate the risks imposed by the strategy and the means of monitoring those risks, and more. In the end the board and management should arrive at a consensus of the corporation's mission and vision for the future—and how to achieve it.

CONCLUSION

The foregoing is a pretty long menu of what I believe can guide directors to build boards that can cope with our capital markets and bring about reform. Detailed as it is, it's necessary to raise the game of directors and value-driven shareholders. Pragmatically, I am proposing a new process for selecting directors and active responses. In the end, directors and shareholders should assess board composition and the corporation's needs while taking proactive steps to build a board that can meet today's challenges. Regulations cannot mandate activist boards. Directors must be the ones to select and recommend members.

I turn again to a seismic event in corporate America, the transformation of the board of General Motors. They went from a great group of men and women doing what was par for the course in those days to an activist board that set the course for future corporate governance: outside directors meeting alone without management, a proactive independent director at the board's helm, and the public firing of an underperforming CEO. Recognize, too, that they were in part prodded by an institutional shareholder.

Nobody around that highly polished table in the boardroom hesitated to ask the tough questions of management.

Corporations face new realities in the vastly changed and changing capital market, including intermediary shareholders of varieties then unknown, wolf-pack attacks by predatory hedge funds on companies with allegedly wobbly financials, instant effects from high-frequency trading, endless news cycles packed with unfiltered commentary, noisy threats from outsiders, and worries that quarterly guidance might be a penny per share off, or that a currency crisis half a world away could send the market into a tailspin. Corporations also face new global competitors, customers and suppliers, and employees who may be replaced because of evolving strategies and technology.

The world around boards is different today. The future of our corporations depends on boards recognizing and adapting to this new landscape.

I have outlined the process for selecting and incentivizing the activist director who recognizes the need for change and partnership with management to safeguard the best interests of the corporation. My hope is that this book provides both the motivation and the means for boards and value shareholders to adapt and ensure the future of their corporations.

AUTHOR'S NOTE

My career has been almost contemporaneous with that of Weil, Gotshal and Manges LLP. I was privileged to start practice in 1951 (figure 1), an era when you were expected to do anything, and your assignments depended on which senior lawyer caught you in the hall. Later we would be "retained" directly by clients. Over time, I did everything that lawyers do: wills, tax returns, reclaiming merchandise, lawsuits for goods sold and delivered, petit jury trials for peanut monies, matrimonials, reading manuscripts for accuracy on behalf of publishers, false advertising cases, copyright matters, counseling basketball and hockey players in their dealings with managements, music licensing, securities antics, bankruptcies, gender issues, not-for-profits, government agencies and authorities (foreign and domestic), airlines, developing countries, representing people I didn't much like during the "red scare," arbitrating cases overseas, overseeing factory test runs in Yugoslavia, attempting to sell a factory to the Indonesian government, a peek at criminal and negligence matters, major and minor antitrust

Figure 1   Antitrust Division of the Department of Justice staff (1951).

counseling and litigation, major and minor board repre-
sentations, dumping, restructuring, partnership disputes,
broadcasting, family matters, fraudulent behavior, retailing,
major and minor mergers and acquisitions, government regulation (local, state, federal), automobiles (manufacturing,
importing), cameras, pharmacies, cigarettes, real estate, and
more. I've taught at Columbia, Yale, Harvard, and NYU
and have done pro bono work for the Central Park Conservancy, the Albert Einstein College of Medicine, the Lower
Manhattan Development Corporation (after September 11)
and the 9/11 Memorial and Museum, the Red Cross, and
many other organizations over the course of more than sixty
years of practice.

When I arrived at Weil in 1951, there were about twenty lawyers. Now there are around eleven hundred in twenty offices around the world. My future long-term partners, Todd Lang and Jesse Wolff, were already there, but the firm, founded in 1931, was really Frank Weil (banking practice), Sylvan Gotshal (retail stores), and Horace Manges (book publishing). Frank was a fatherly figure who took a great interest in my personal development and was the reason I joined the firm.

We didn't really bill our time at first. When we finished a case, we'd just all sit down and say, "Well, what was it worth?" Frank or Sylvan would pick a number based on knowledge of the client and a rough estimate of how much time we spent, since we didn't keep time sheets. Then one of them would say, "Well, that was worth ten thousand dollars." Or whatever. In those days, ten thousand dollars was big money.

Compensation also seemed somewhat arbitrary, at least in the beginning. It certainly wasn't transparent. During one phase, Sylvan Gotshal would make all compensation decisions, based on a secretive "black book" approach tied to the clients you produced for the firm. This was a method that Todd, Jesse, and I dispensed with when we took over management of the firm in 1974. It wasn't conducive to teamwork.

While I am no longer part of firm management, today the process is essentially unchanged from what we adopted back then. Client work is one of many factors Weil considers when determining partner compensation. We also consider leadership, community concerns, philanthropic activities, and firm-mindedness activities. It's transparent. In my view, how compensation is handled is the foundation of trust among the partners, and for that matter, within any organization where cooperation is essential. Greed and opaqueness at the top do not engender long-term success—anywhere. I think we handled compensation fairly and earned that trust. The firm thrived.

There have been periods when the collaborative culture was in jeopardy. The threat of a me-me-me environment is at times very real. It has fallen to Barry Wolf, who became executive partner and chair of the management committee in 2010, to protect the culture that Todd, Jesse, and I spent decades creating. I have full confidence that Barry will continue in a preeminent international law firm, upholding the firm's culture and values, including encouraging young partners and associates to become involved with nonprofit boards, pro bono work, and other civic activities. It's part of what has made the Weil culture different from many New York law firms.

Early on I gained the reputation that I was demanding. It was said that if I didn't fire you at least once, you would never make partner. I never really fired anybody. I would just get angry and say, "You're fired." Donald Trump has commercialized the words, but he meant it, I didn't. People I "fired" eventually became partners, except maybe one or two. There was one who missed an important update in the law, rendering erroneous my presentation to a client—which was embarrassing to the firm. But then there was an unfortunate associate who forgot to file a brief with the federal court. I was before the judge, who asked a relevant question. I assured him that it was addressed in my reply brief.

The judge said, "What reply brief?" I turned around and glared at the lawyer who was supposed to have filed it. He turned ashen, but I forgave him—it was a very good brief and I presented it orally.

My staff has learned to cope with me over the years. One of my most trusted assistants, Sally Sasso, has worked with me since 1979 when she was in high school and worked at Weil part time. Told not to disturb me, she once took a message from a potential client, and I remonstrated her when she gave me the note later. "So now *you're* deciding which clients I take?" I spoke a bit loudly. Sally went home in tears to her father, who was sympathetic but practical, explaining that this was a valuable learning experience and to just go back to work the next day. That was more than thirty-five years ago, and she's still here. Now she is not just my assistant, but also my good and trusted friend.

A few events stand out in my mind that shaped the lawyer I am today and laid the foundation for Weil to become a premier law firm. These are beyond the matters I describe in this book to illustrate corporate governance issues.

One is my involvement in the 1963 Great Salad Oil Swindle and our representation of Ira Haupt & Co., at the time a fine Wall Street brokerage house. American Express had recently created a new division that specialized in field warehousing that lent to businesses using inventories as collateral. This included writing warehouse receipts to Tino De Angelis for millions of dollars' worth of vegetable oil. There were hundreds of millions of dollars in warehouse receipts signed by American Express. In addition, De Angelis had an operative steal a bunch of blank warehouse receipts from American

Express Warehousing. They were forged to show that there were large quantities of salad oil in American Express storage tanks. For both types of receipts, the tanks were filled mostly with water and only a thin, constantly replenished layer of oil on top, to foil any inspectors. There was also a complicated series of pipes that could move real salad oil from tank to tank if the inspectors were there. Ultimately, Haupt went bankrupt b'ecause it held the receipts, and had bankrolled De Angelis in his trading.

Charles Seligson, mentioned in earlier sections of this book, trustee in bankruptcy for Haupt and a recognized bankruptcy expert in the United States, hired Weil to represent him in claims against those who had helped De Angelis. Seligson taught at NYU and his book on bankruptcy is still the leading treatise on the subject. "The Professor," as everyone called him, was impressed by my pitch to represent Haupt but concerned about whether we had the staff to handle it. "We were not Sullivan & Cromwell or Cravath," my partner Carl Lobell notes. In fact it was just me, Carl, and Irving Scher in our little group, a disclosure I deftly avoided. I persuaded the Professor that we would draw people from all of our different departments. "Ira can sell anything," Carl is fond of saying.

On behalf of Haupt, we brought a case against American Express Warehousing on a unique theory of liability that practically all of Wall Street—and their law firms—rejected as irrelevant. We argued that American Express knew or should have known that De Angelis was a thief and therefore should have taken precautions to prevent the theft. That's an accepted concept in tort law, but not in a contracts case, which this was. The trustee had $7.4 million in forged receipts, and we wound up getting $2.5 million, a good settlement in a case that had been treated as meritless.

That case gave Weil visibility and we entered a practice area we hadn't been much in before—Wall Street.

The biggest benefit, however, was that we happily convinced the Professor to become our partner, though initially my senior partners resisted on the grounds that bankruptcy was not a mainstream practice, and indeed, not considered reputable. "We'll never represent another bank!" was the argument. "That's ridiculous. We don't represent any banks now. What are we talking about?" I said. "No, that's out of the question," said an elder. "I don't want to discuss it."

Dejected, I went back into my office, where my then-secretary Sarah Schulman, an older very motherly lady, seeing my distress, asked what happened. When I told her, she said, "That's silly. You go back and tell them you're doing it." I said, "I can't." She said, "Go back and tell them you are."

So I walked back to the group, and nervously but firmly said, "I don't accept this. We should take Seligson. This is a chance of a lifetime!" Thanks in large part to Sarah, they finally gave in and Seligson joined the firm, soon to be followed by his partner Harvey Miller, who became a bankruptcy legend, and a key to the firm's growth.

At the time, Wall Street was in trouble with financially shaky real estate investment trusts. Harvey, who had earned the respect of several banks with his work as a trustee with Seligson in the Haupt bankruptcy, was retained by Chase Manhattan Bank on referral from the Rockefeller bank's law firm, Milbank, Tweed. It was a turning point for the firm.

Figure 2 Weil, Gotshal and Manges partnership (1955).

Not only did we develop a solid, very best, long-lasting bankruptcy practice, we also established relationships with several large banks.

I grew a quite successful antitrust practice. We represented GE, J. C. Penney, Westinghouse, American Airlines, GM, and the United States government in major antitrust and trade regulation affairs. I became chairman of the Antitrust Law Sections of both the New York State Bar and American Bar Associations (figure 2).

At one point, three of us—Harvey Miller (bankruptcy), Todd Lang (corporate), and I (antitrust/trade regulation)— represented the bulk of the firm's practice. Of course none of us would have succeeded without the support of terrific partners who could eventually take over our practices. Today it is different. There are many individual partners who have developed or maintained substantial practices. This of course requires the hard work and dedication of a growing number of attorneys.

With the presidency of Ronald Reagan and the advent of market theory in the '80s, major antitrust matters waned. These laws were embargoed. I wondered how, without enforcement, corporate behavior would be restrained? I was teaching courses on topics close to corporate governance, which led me to understand the new capital markets and how they impacted the behavior of corporations. Enter corporate governance, now of more importance to me—supposedly the governor of interrelationships between corporations and investors. Harvey and I urged the firm to build a financial sector practice, in addition to our successful bankruptcy, reorganization, litigation, regular corporate, and antitrust practices. Wachtell, Lipton and Skadden, Arps had done that. It was the takeover era. Skadden represented the raiders. Wachtell played defense. It worked beautifully, and both firms prospered.

It was late for us, but other firms like Cravath and Sullivan had caught up. We could too. By that time Harvey, Todd, and I had turned over firm management to Stephen Dannhauser. It was time. He led us in developing a financial sector practice. To become a force in the financial sector took patience, some critical lateral hires, and in-house to firm-lawyer conversions. By dint of an overall team effort, where everyone pitched in as our culture made possible, the firm has made itself a go-to law firm in M&A, private equity, and other key elements of the financial/legal market.

I am most proud of my partners who, often selflessly, have always pitched in to innovate and grow the firm. We had decided the firm was to be an "institution," not simply a collection of talented individual practitioners. Note that the name has never changed.

That's how I thrived, a firm grew, and a culture developed to encourage it all. A culture which, looking back, has formed the basis of my corporate governance counseling from the beginning. For that I am grateful.

I learned too that close ties to top executives were helpful in other ways. One client was American Airlines. I was close to its CEO and chairman, Albert Casey. He was the leader of another client of ours, Times Mirror, before joining American Airlines. I would later play a more involved role advising the airline when it was blindsided by a flight attendants strike a week before Thanksgiving 1993. That event created a public relations nightmare for the carrier, and was resolved only when President Clinton persuaded both sides to agree to binding arbitration to settle the increasingly bitter dispute.

But almost fifteen years earlier, in May 1979, my relationship with Casey proved especially useful. I was enjoying one of the four first-class seats on American flight 293 from New York to Chicago, en route to an important (to me) oral argument before a federal judge. A man, a Serbian nationalist it turned out, stormed by me and into the cockpit. In a thick Eastern European accent, the man said, "I have bomb. We go to Chicago." "Sit down," said the pilot. "We *are* going to Chicago!"

It's unusual to hijack a plane to its intended destination. But he threatened to blow up the plane if a certain Serbian priest in a Chicago jail was not released. He was carrying, in fact, what appeared to be pipe bombs. Coincidentally the flight attendant, who performed admirably in assessing the situation and calming us all, was the daughter of a close friend.

After circling for what seemed to be an interminable amount of time, the plane almost ran out of fuel, landed at O'Hare, and taxied to a remote part of the airport. FBI agents dressed as mechanics started milling around the plane. It seemed clear to me that if the passengers weren't released soon, the agents would likely storm the plane, which I feared would be a fatal mistake. At best, the would-be bomber seemed unstable and unpredictable.

As the cabin filled with banjo music and the smell of marijuana from a bunch of students in the back, seemingly unaware of what was happening and having a good time, the hijacker was getting jittery. I insisted through the flight attendant that the pilot help me let Casey know about the "storming." Given the situation, the hijacker appeared perplexed that a white-haired passenger from first class tried to speak to the pilot. I tried to communicate with everyone not to storm the plane. If that happened, I thought, he would blow us all up and I would be personally upset with everyone involved (after the fact?).

Incidentally, during the delays, I wrote a letter to my family describing my affection for them, and the like, forgetting that such a letter would disappear if there were an explosion.

Happily, negotiations resolved the matter. The passengers were released.

Another time, being close to the CEO had real drawbacks—a lesson I learned while advising the chairman of Macy's, Ed Finkelstein, a brilliant merchant who had transformed the retailer's dowdy 34th Street flagship into a worthy competitor to Bloomingdales, its flashy cross-town rival run by Marvin Traub.

After working together for years on transactional and governance matters, Ed and I were good friends. We had vacationed together with our families and saw each other regularly outside the office. And that was the problem. I had fallen under Ed's spell, as had his handpicked board, which included Henry Kissinger and Beverly Sills.

Ed had done a splendid job of expanding Macy's, but had accrued a huge pile of debt, which the company couldn't cover. In 1986, worried about a hostile takeover, Ed led a $3.5 billion leveraged buyout of the company. To celebrate, he staged a lavish gala at the Metropolitan Museum of Art, with buglers and drummers. I had doubts about Macy's spending so much money. But, caught up in the euphoria, I went along. I even made a speech at the gala about how wonderful it all was, which, unfortunately, I believed. Ed and his family were pleased.

Then Ed spent even more money: $1 billion two years later to buy the Bullocks and I. Magnin chains from Federated Department Stores. It seemed like a good idea, but by 1990 Macy's had $4 billion in long-term debt, and rumors of bankruptcy circulated. At a board meeting where there should have been a serious discussion of the debt crisis, Ed put on a lingerie show with live models. There was no debate. It may have been the one meeting when every male member of the board paid rapt attention. The directors, mesmerized, had substituted faith and *traditional support* for a charismatic leader. I had let myself become part of the scenery.

Two years later Macy's announced an indefinite delay in paying suppliers. The company filed for bankruptcy soon after, and the board replaced Ed. I had looked the other way, and vowed never again to get too close to my clients or allow affection to cloud the role that lawyers, inside and out, must play.

Those are experiences I bring to counseling those who are the core of corporate governance—managers, directors, and investors. They are people I try to understand, and maybe I understand them better because of my past. I learned too that friendships with clients would help in some circumstances, but were not to cloud my judgment. I have survived good times and very challenging times. Practicing law in an enabling law firm, I truly had the overall benefit of engaging in just about every aspect of being a lawyer. Counseling in corporate governance incorporated all of these experiences.

ACKNOWLEDGMENTS

It would be impossible to acknowledge everyone by name who generously contributed time and effort so that this book could be written, for I talked endlessly with many about where I was headed. I will, however, name and thank a few who inspired me, encouraged me, and helped me along the way. I owe them a sincere public thank you.

I am grateful to Stewart Pinkerton, a distinguished author and editor whose career spans *The Wall Street Journal* and *Forbes*, for his research, advice on storytelling, and general guidance. I am also grateful to my editor Stephen Wesley, who focused the manuscript, and to Myles Thompson of Columbia University Press, who saw merit in the original manuscript. Thanks as well to Weil, Gotshal & Manges senior associate Aabha Sharma, who patiently and substantively navigated me through the maze of memory, advice, writing, and editing; and to Sally Sasso, my assistant of over thirty years, who was able to find files, recall names, and lay the groundwork for so much; and to Ian Jackman, Kara Welsh, and Martin Levin from the publishing world for holding my hand throughout the process. Thank you to my wife Susan Frame Millstein, who insisted that I put my head down and get the book done, and who counseled me along the way.

There are those who played instrumental roles in the stories I share throughout this book and those who helped me bring these stories to life . . . who deserve mention in an honor roll of patience: Harry Pearce and Robert Pugliesi, both general counsels who from their respective positions kept me on track; John Zuccotti, my dear friend and confidant; Harvey Goldschmid, Columbia University professor, lifetime friend, and co-teacher at Columbia Law School; Paul MacAvoy, the most professional professor with whom I co-authored earlier articles and a book grounding this one, who guided me through the strange world of academia; Howard Rubenstein, with whom I could laugh and delight in the arcane world we live in; and Mats Isaksson of the OECD, with whom I learned of the governance world outside of the United States.

I am indebted to David Nierenberg, who partnered with me in nurturing and intellectually stimulating a center devoted to corporate governance at Yale and continuing at Columbia. I am also indebted to William McCracken, retired CEO and chair of CA Technologies, who brought it back from the brink, and with his invaluable hands-on experiences and our many hours of discussion, brought the concept of the activist director to life; and to my son Jim Millstein for his financial expertise; and to Richard Brodsky and David Kidera, with whom I fought the wars of fiduciary duties for government entities; and to Governor George Pataki, who entrusted me to chair task forces to start the process of building integrity in government; and to Steve Ifshin for his practical advice.

I thank the partners at Weil who have worked side by side with me, either on matters described in this book, or by collaborating, debating, and making me the lawyer I am today. They gave me their time and expertise: Barry Wolf, Harvey Miller, Richard Davis, Carl Lobell, Alan Miller, Robert Messineo, Alan Weinschel, Steven Reiss, Greg Danilow, and Stephen Radin. I also want to thank the indefatigable staff of Weil library and records department.

Finally, in recounting people involved in my stories—except for a few publicly identified as persons who tripped over the line—the bulk were ordinary people, human beings doing what may have been par for the course in their times. There were no villains.